AT TWELVE

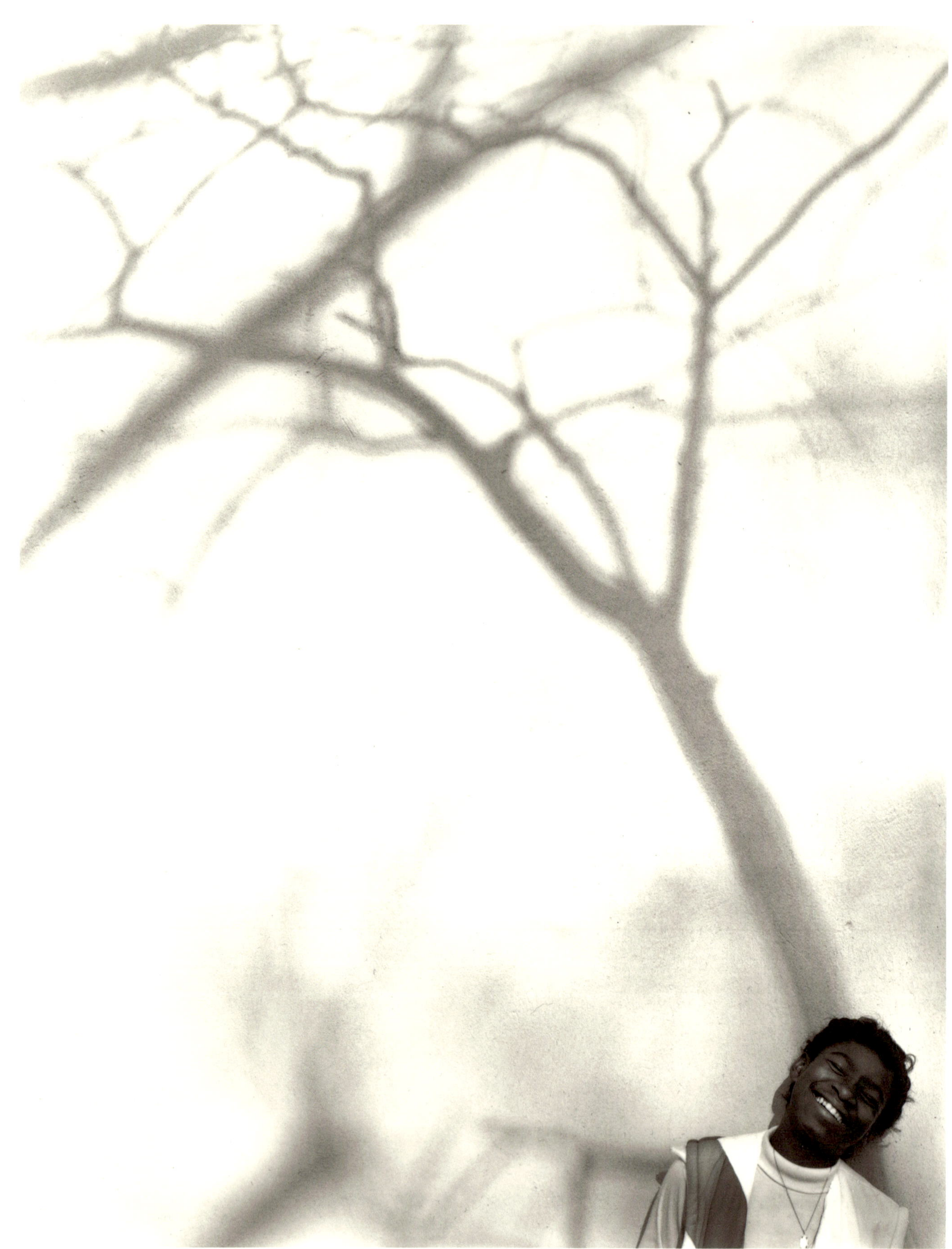

AT TWELVE

PORTRAITS OF YOUNG WOMEN

BY SALLY MANN

Introduction by Ann Beattie

APERTURE

Aperture Foundation gratefully acknowledges support for this publication from the Sydney and Frances Lewis Foundation.

The staff for this book at Aperture Foundation includes:
Michael E. Hoffman, *Executive Director*; Steve Dietz, *Editor*; Lisa Rosset, *Managing Editor*; Stevan A. Baron, *Production Director*; Jason Greenberg, Tessa Lowinsky, *Editorial Work Scholars*. Book design by Christy Hale.

Printed by Agit Mariogros Industrie Grafiche Srl, Beinasco - Turin, Italy
20 19 18 17 16 15 14 13 12 11 10 9 8

Library of Congress Control Number: 87-071950
Hardcover ISBN 978-0-89381-296-6
Paperback ISBN 978-0-89381-330-7

Aperture Foundation books are available in North America through:
D.A.P./Distributed Art Publishers
155 Sixth Avenue, 2nd Floor
New York, N.Y. 10013
Phone: (212) 627-1999
Fax: (212) 627-9484

Aperture Foundation books are distributed outside North America by:
Thames & Hudson
181A High Holborn
London WC1V 7QX
United Kingdom
Phone: + 44 20 7845 5000
Fax: + 44 20 7845 5055
Email: sales@thameshudson.co.uk

aperturefoundation
547 West 27th Street
New York, N.Y. 10001
www.aperture.org

The purpose of Aperture Foundation, a non-profit organization, is to advance photography in all its forms and to foster the exchange of ideas among audiences worldwide.

This book is for Larry, for his kindness and his intelligence and his great and generous heart.

And for my children, Emmett, Jessie and, eventually, Virginia, who accompanied me on these photographic forays as uncomplaining friends and unwaveringly direct critics.

We Are Their Mirror, They Are Ours

by Ann Beattie

Look at the eyes. It is as if we are looking at them, but they are *seeing* us. Though Sally Mann may have located what seemed to be the appropriate background, asked that an adjustment be made or an object with symbolic connotations moved into the frame, there is no way she could have requested the look in their eyes.

The harder we study these photographs, the more it seems that Mann's subjects are where they should not be. Yet how can one say "should not" when this is the twelve year old's environment, when the behavior of the adults is beyond the girl's control, when another washday is as ordinary as the chair in which the girl sits.

Many of the girls look at the camera straight-on, happy to appear in their finery or willing to participate in a picture that will be made of them in their world, all judgment aside. Mann must have communicated to the girls that she wasn't judging them—or, at the very least, that there were no consequences. After all: artists pick up paintbrushes or cameras instead of gavels because pronouncements aren't of primary importance to them. Art is an exploration. And considering the evidence in this book, the artist has done a lot of looking around, spent a long time contemplating her subjects. In most cases, it is obvious that the subjects were both aware of the photographer and at the same time relaxed. This is quite miraculous. Because young people are great sensors of dishonesty, I have to assume that Mann must have gained their trust by being very forthright in the way she presented herself. It no doubt worked to her advantage that she was photographing them in their worlds, rather than in a studio. At times, it may have helped that children seem to feel that one thing is not much more important than another: a photograph is just a picture somebody wants to take.

Interpreting photographs is another matter. Anyone who has studied his or her own family snapshots will know that, quite often, some surprising revelation may be found in the studio-like picture of Aunt Mildred, sitting with her hands clasped, and that something mysterious or truly lovely may show up in the quick shot of Uncle Bobby putting the first steak on the barbecue grill. In providing us with something unexpected, twelve year olds are no different from adults. But when the girls are photographed, I think we register their postures, self-betrayals, and exuberance differently. While we empathize with their qualities, they are children, after all: we still feel an urge to protect them. While for them looking into a camera lens is analogous to looking into a mirror, what they mirror for the viewer, with their attitudes and their dead-on eye contact, is us. We are their mirror, they are ours.

When a girl is twelve years old, she often wants—or says she wants—less involvement with adults. It's a pretty hands-off time between parents and children, a time in which the girls yearn for freedom and adults feel their own grip on things becoming a little tenuous, as they realize that they have to let their children go. The dynamic changes. But I think the fascination remains the same—the fact that, as the girls grow, the parents have to acknowledge that their little girl is becoming something (not someone) else, and that means they may become something else, too.

In Mann's remarks on the circumstances surrounding these photographs, we can read much between the lines about why these subjects captivated her attention, and even about how she decided what seemed true and necessary to communicate about the roles the girls are playing midway between the gropings of childhood and the rigors and regrets of adulthood. Twelve-year-old girls know what brought them to the present moment, but that's as far as they've gotten. Their guesses and desires strongly emerge in these photographs. In many, the world of childhood (or the realization that it has been left behind so abruptly) seems very apparent; in others, the girls' comportment seems humorously, or soberingly, adult. In looking so much like us, they can seem parodic or unnerving. In any case, what we see seems so real—so much as though the photographer captured them in a fishbowl—that it represents a state of awareness that will never be escaped, however it may be altered as time passes.

Most photographers will tell you that they look for significant, rather than ultimate, moments for revelations. In this collection of photographs, we view subjects who, either willingly or without suspecting, have been positioned in blatant or symbolic contexts. But whether the girls have been set in place or quickly captured, their existence retains a certain mystery that is not easily assessed. Sometimes they seem to have been caught off-guard. More often, it is their composure and dignity that seems to make them transcendent. Though standing on a ladder, the dark-haired girl photographed in front of the painting of a Civil War battle gives the illusion of moving quickly past. The photographer could not have anticipated the girl's particular emotion, although she must have been acting on a hunch about how a painting and a particular subject could reflect one another. In this case, the girl's expression seems both vulnerable and formidable. The blurriness makes her ghostlike; she is someone who is about to escape the picture frame, it seems, but she will not escape without having made a significant impression.

While the painting is in a way transformed by the girl's presence, and as a backdrop it may be revelatory of something about the girl, only the simple-minded could see it as an explanation of her character. Likewise, the girl stretched on the hood of a car, resting behind the word "DOOM" scrawled in the dust, is stopped by the camera, made prisoner to her situation. Because of proximity, each is understood in terms of some nearby object—but that painting or car hood is also understood in relation to the girls. My feeling is that rather than coming to know these people in terms of the context in which they are depicted, the context only serves to complicate our response.

In Sally Mann's photographs everything that we see matters. The photograph of the blond girl sitting beside the front steps is an example of a portrait changed many times by everything and everyone else included in the frame. Seated apart from the others, the girl on the left knows—or means to assert—that this is *her* portrait. And so it stays, because of and in spite of the others. Though the younger girl sitting on the steps, toes turned inward, thinks that the portrait might as well be hers, and though two others watch the photographer, our eye keeps returning to the person whose comportment makes it clear that she is the star of the show. If the out-of-focus leaves of the tree were a curtain that had just risen on a Broadway stage, you could be no clearer about the star, and you could make some quick assumptions about the roles the other characters would play. It's a mystery, that star's quality of straightforward involvement mixed with self-containment (hand draped over the railing, legs parted). The others all seem to be curious, as if the photographer might speak to them or give them some answer, but the girl on the left is not questioning anything. She's decided to give something, and once decided upon there isn't another question to ask. Then our eye begins to observe detail. Whose shoes are they, on the pathway, that seem to have been suddenly abandoned? That person is gone: where and why? As we begin to wonder, our eye will go back repeatedly to the center of the world we're trying to figure out: the girl on the left who, always provocative, becomes increasingly enigmatic, the center of attention in spite of the cluster of children on the right, or the mystery person who simply stepped out of his shoes and went away.

The details are important. Notice the child's empty car in the photograph of the girl with the wash, and the butterfly net under the arm of the girl lying on the car. Or the corner of the birdcage seen in the portrait-within-a-portrait (two sisters photographed with a framed portrait that depicts a romanticized conception of childhood in days gone by). The parameters of these children's worlds must sometimes make them feel claustrophobic (they seem to know that, and even carry props that embody their own entrapment). Butterfly nets, a garden hose that circles the ground like a lasso, and a piece of fabric stretched over a person's chest like a bondage tie may at first glance seem like simple things, but because of our experiences they take on added significance. As adults, we see what the children may not see. We are the ones who have provided them with a particular world, yet we have little control over how they use the props, or when they assume our postures. In quite a few of Mann's photographs the obvious leaps out at us: the girl in front of her playhouse, a man behind her, his face obliterated by shadow, towering there as the force of darkness. We quickly realize how intrusive adults can be, that adults can step into a child's world and dwarf it, as the furniture is dwarfed in the photograph. These girls have seen enough of the postures and affectations of adults to approximate or mimic them successfully. Our response to this is complicated, however, because we see where these acts have gotten us. Is the world in which the girls exist really an innocent world in which a pose is only a pose? Paradoxically, we find that the cumulative effect of these photographs is that the danger is often implied by the adults themselves, whether it is suggested by the seemingly harmless grip of an arm, or in the futility implied by a supportive arm dropped low, enfolding the child on the lap but clearly failing to hold her attention in the adult world.

The obvious risk for the photographer when working with symbols is that the person being photographed may disappear under the weight of the message, though it seems clear that Mann's subjects transcend being understood in merely symbolic terms. Once we label something as symbolic, we are dealing in an abstraction, yet the reality of so many young faces seems so intense, so concrete, and the prints so clear, that we feel sure we have something real before us. Sally Mann acknowledges symbols—even adjusts things to compose the shots—but although we see the connection (the objects and details are hardly covert; our eye goes instantly to them), we continue to study the photographs because there still seems to be a larger life to the people in them. The girl with the dark circles under her eyes, backed up against the floral-patterned drapery wears a dress that is not very pretty, really—more like an odd improvisation on children's flowered dresses—and becomes increasingly strange as we sense that it functions as protective coloration. If it protects her (which is doubtful to begin with, since children suffer the tortures of the damned when they do not look just like everyone else), we can't imagine how. Pictorially, Mann is expressing a figure of speech: this girl is the person who fades into the wallpaper. But in spite of her attire, and in spite of the surroundings which nearly subsume her, the eyes have depth. The circles beneath them let us know that much is wrong. So dressed, the child might have vanished if Mann had not stopped to look. Similarly, if you look at the girl standing inside the charmed circle of the garden hose, it seems certain that the photographer saw how perfect the loop was. At the moment of the photograph, though, flanked by boys who either see her as a catch or will eventually see her as a catch, the girl transcends being a person caught in a symbolic situation; hands in her pockets, adopting a casual stance, it's easy to see that she is deliberately facing down the photographer (and by extension, all viewers). An outsider has to wonder what the dynamic will be when the boys, too, move out of their postures and begin to interact with the girl. We have before us an image that tells us something about what the present moment is in the girl's life, and that makes us imagine her future.

Consider the two girls sitting at the base of a tree that, split and repaired, now looks like a vagina in brick and bark. Though the girls probably did not see the sexual implications of the background, the photographer did, and because of that the viewer cannot help but interpret the girls in terms of the tree. Their pose is also casual, relaxed, a posture that would not rivet all eyes to their crotches had the girls not been positioned this way. The picture *is* a set-up, but because we see the symbol so quickly—because an assessment has already been made—we back off and begin to decide things for ourselves. We study everything more intently than we might have had the tree not initially diverted us. Finally, the girls transcend their proximity to the tree in part because we *want* them to transcend it.

It can be very clear, early on, who will transcend circumstances and who will not. A sense of humor helps, and looking at some of these photographs we smile, I think, because the subjects who smile for the camera seem to tacitly acknowledge that they are amused by what they are doing. The girl in a formal dress, atop a pedestal, has seen other pictures of beauty queens and knows what pose to take. She knows that she's young, though, and not a real beauty queen: subject and audience are in on this joke together. The pedestal/sundial is too small a surface to allow for anything but a brief moment of glory. As we study her—outdoors, instead of on a runway—we begin to sense the precariousness of her pose, and her vulnerability. Does she suppose that this momentary presentation can prevail in the larger world? Yet it's fun—you can look at her and know she was happy to have her picture taken this way—and she doesn't mind being very open about her looks: a pretty girl, pleasing her audience. The moment before the photograph was taken must have been humorous, and the moment of descent will no doubt be equally tentative, but for the time of the picture the subject and audience are united in suspended disbelief. In some ways, this image seems connected to the photograph of the girl who stands with the blood-stained laundry behind her, stretching a stocking across her chest. What she seems to be saying to the photographer and audience is: We're both mocking something, right? Is this naughty-but-nice expression what you want? Her face lets us know that she sees there's something amusing and excessive about her pose. It's as though she's asking whether she can taunt us this way and still have us on her side, whether the suggestion of bondage isn't rather appropriate in this context. She might as well be telling us that we're all in this thing—all in this photograph—together.

It seems to me that here, and elsewhere in Mann's photographs, we *are* complicitous. We look back to childhood wanting to see aspects of ourselves that we might have forgotten, repressed, or abandoned, yet often what we see is not an ideal childhood, but a world typified by stains on the sheets. The horse's legs were broken, or our faces registered the shadows of broken glass. Or at times, exhilarated, we cast shadows as if, standing at the base of a tree, we stood at the beginning of a rainbow and it rose right out of our heads.

Sally Mann's photographs don't glamorize the world, but they don't make it into something more unpleasant than it is, either. Childhood and adolescence are resonant, significant, and sometimes symbolic—yet the photographer never gives us the idea that her subjects can be relegated to operatives in some myth that can easily be contained in the moment. In their routines and parodies, they are far more complex. We will be amused and a little uneasy to see the narcissistic rapture exhibited by the girl with the billowing, pseudo-wedding veil, clasping the phallic bottle of Tab to her body. In many cases, we may wish that these moments would endure, and be frustrated to realize that they will not. Other times what we see—the girl on the bed, her own infant beside her and her toy doll collection shelved—may be too painful, too much of the real world, to willingly confront. In all cases, though, the undeniable physicality of these girls overpowers the viewer. In these photographs we see so many expectant faces, so much preening, so many long legs parted or prancing or drawn in to the chest for protection, that it would be wonderful if we could reach out and touch the girls who are so real. Their worlds have become still for the moment of the photograph, stopped long enough for us to really consider them. Yet time after time any impulse to interact with them is blocked. Their demeanor stops us: we're made uncomfortable as we consider intruding in anyone else's rapturous trance. In some instances, the girls have so much self-containment that we hesitate, reluctant to move forward; in others, they are laughing, in control of the joke.

There are many ways to consider these photographs. They are, I believe, cautionary. Images are not answers. Yet, like shadows, photographs do tie things together. Consider the two sisters, lounging with a painting of old-fashioned girls, the present-day world and the world of the past made contiguous by shadow. Or the patterns made by light and dark in the photograph of the girl standing on the hanging bridge, the stream of sunlight illuminating her on life's path which is, in childhood and adulthood, suspended over fast-moving water. Those moments that make us pause can allow us to make sense of things, sometimes, just as fast as the camera lens clicks.

Though the girls are shown vulnerable in their youthfulness—even victimized in some instances—the photographer is interested in the strength they possess. They will look hard at the camera because they are used to looking hard at people and things, and because they are already quite accustomed to intruders. Some of the girls are privileged and some are survivors, but in all cases: the photographer has had to make a split-second decision to capture the moment when the subject has done something truly revelatory. If the photographer is right, then the limitations of the orchestrated moment will have been overcome. That, it seems, is the exhilirating moment for all artists.

What knowing watchfulness in the eyes of a twelve year old . . . at once guarded, yet guileless. She is the very picture of contradiction: on the one hand diffident and ambivalent, on the other forthright and impatient; half pertness and half pout. She disarms me with her sure sense of her own attractiveness and, with it, her direct, even provocative approach to the camera. Impossibly, she is both artless and sophisticated; a child and yet a woman.

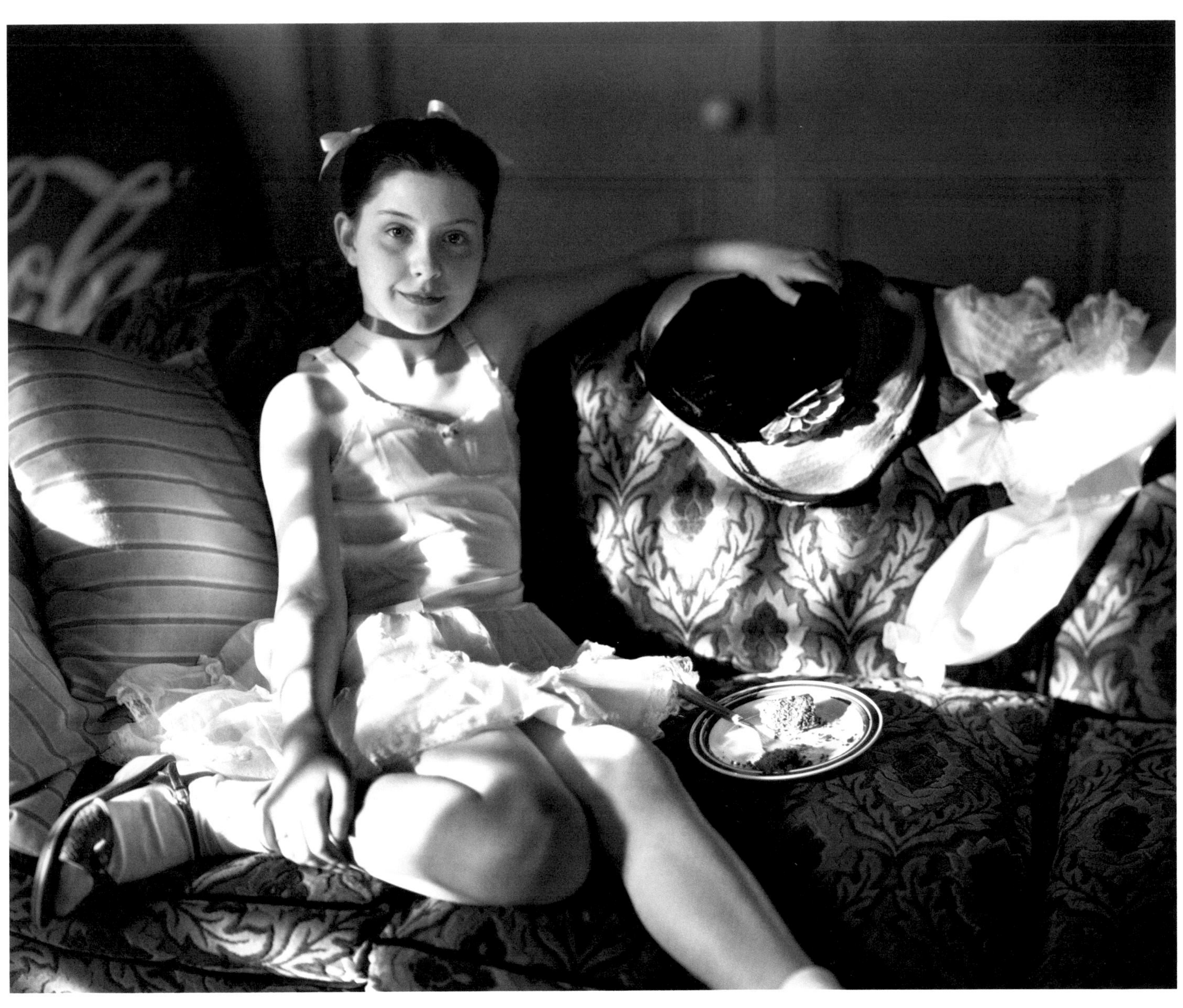

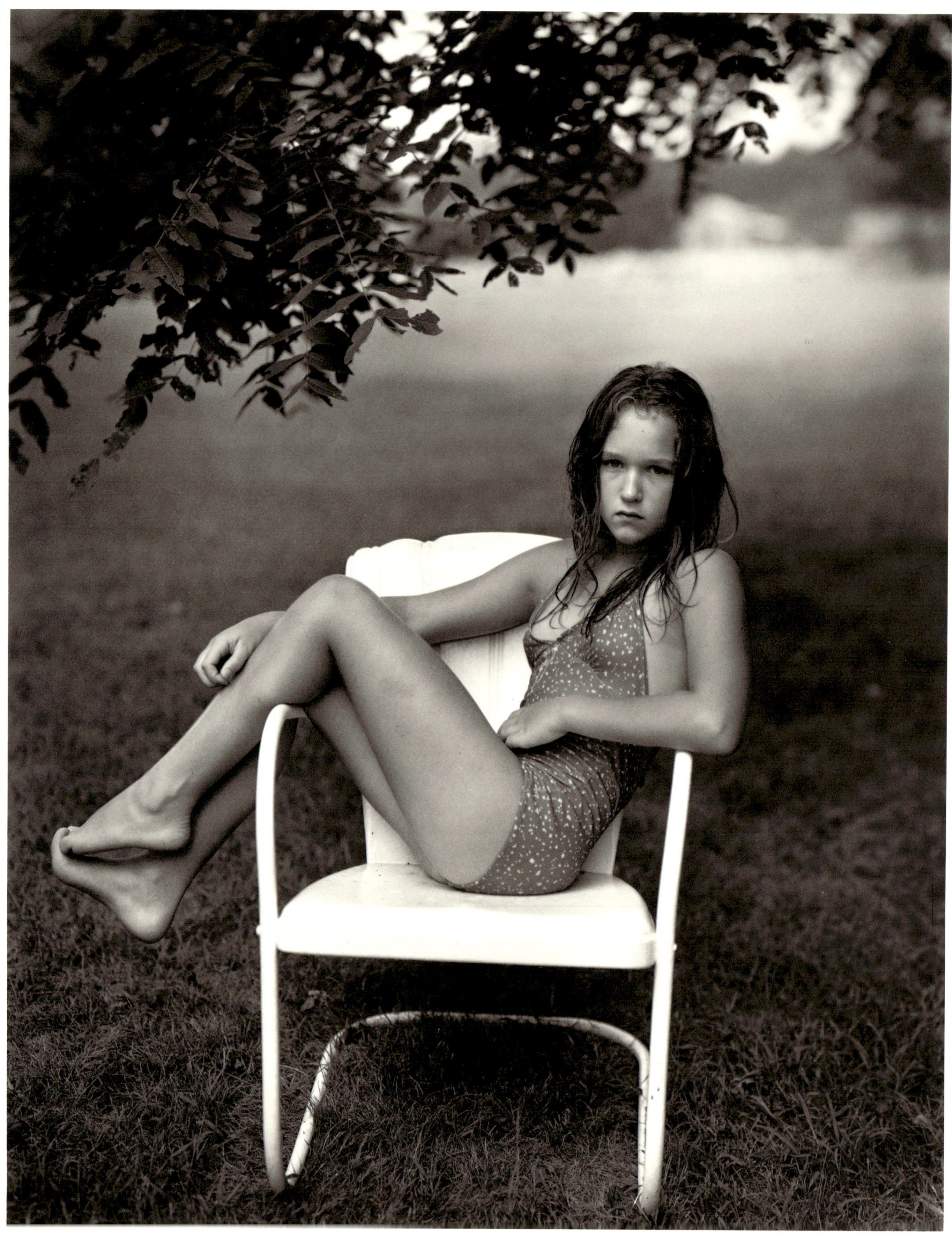

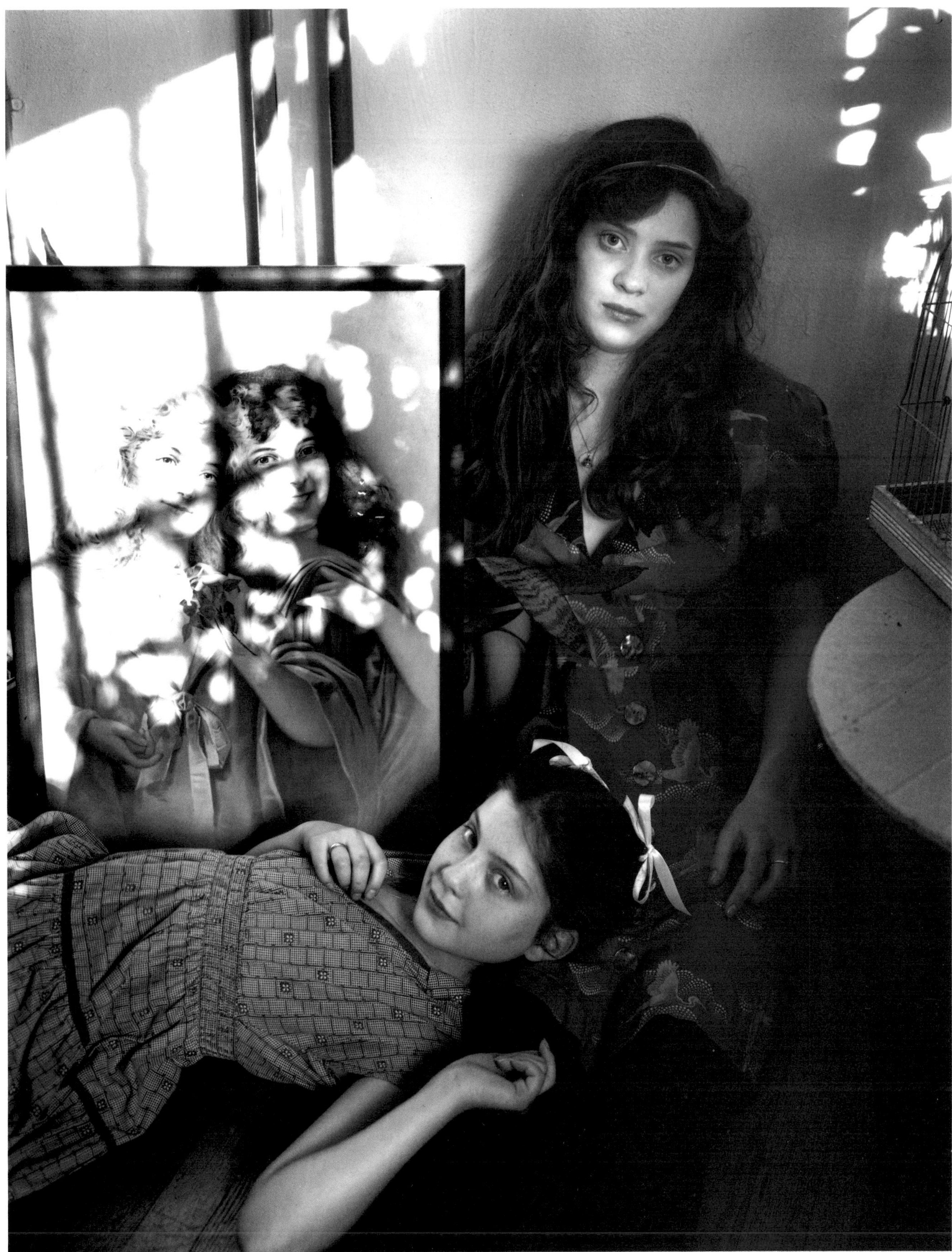

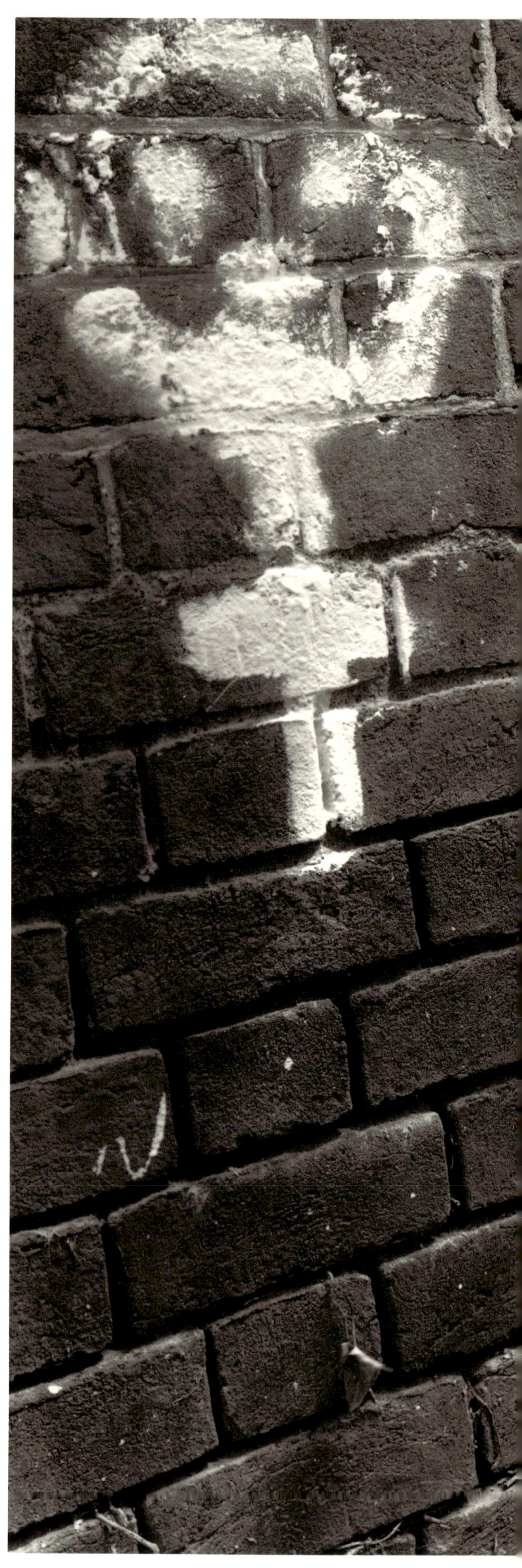

The only girl on the boy's summer softball team.

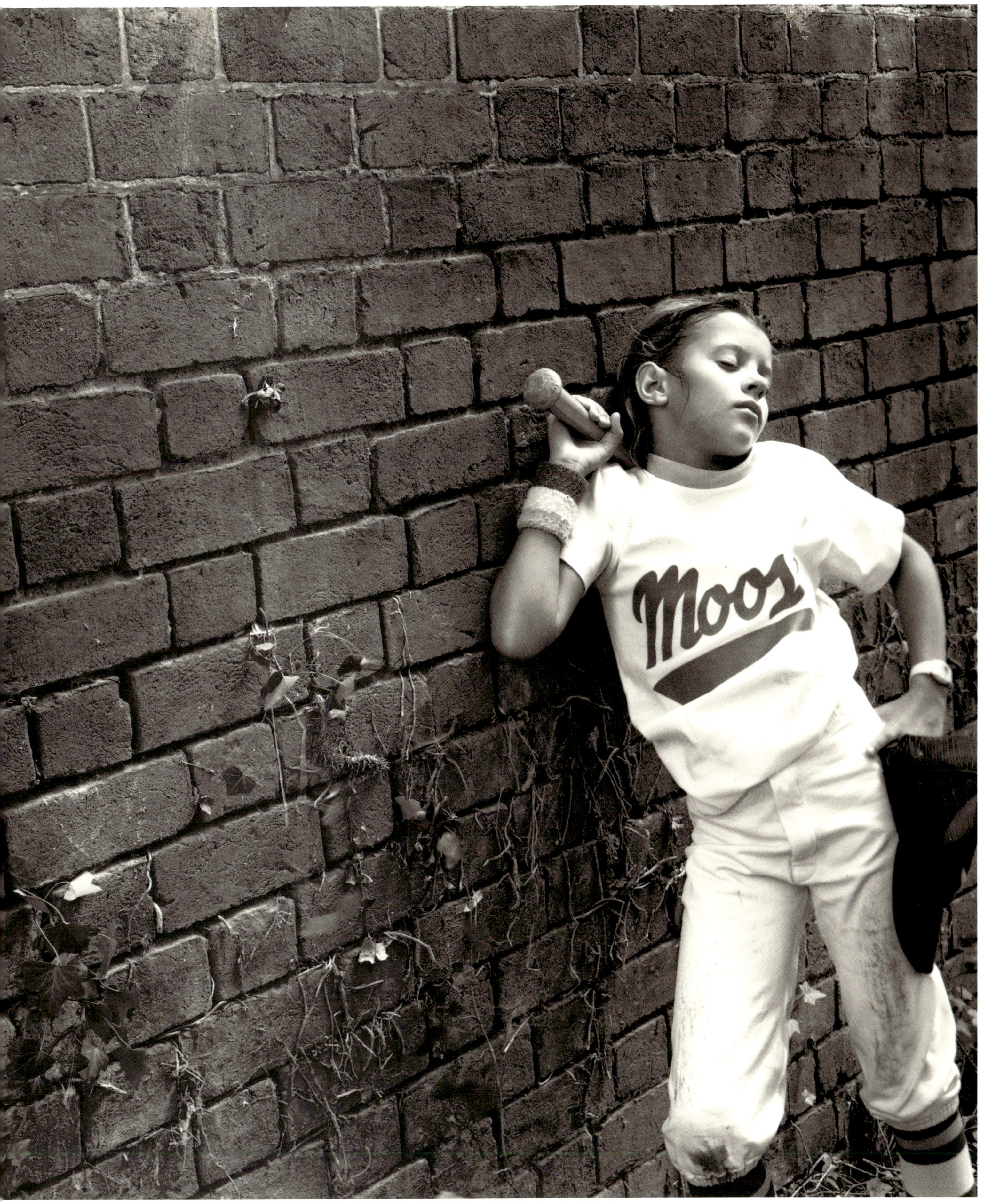
Moos

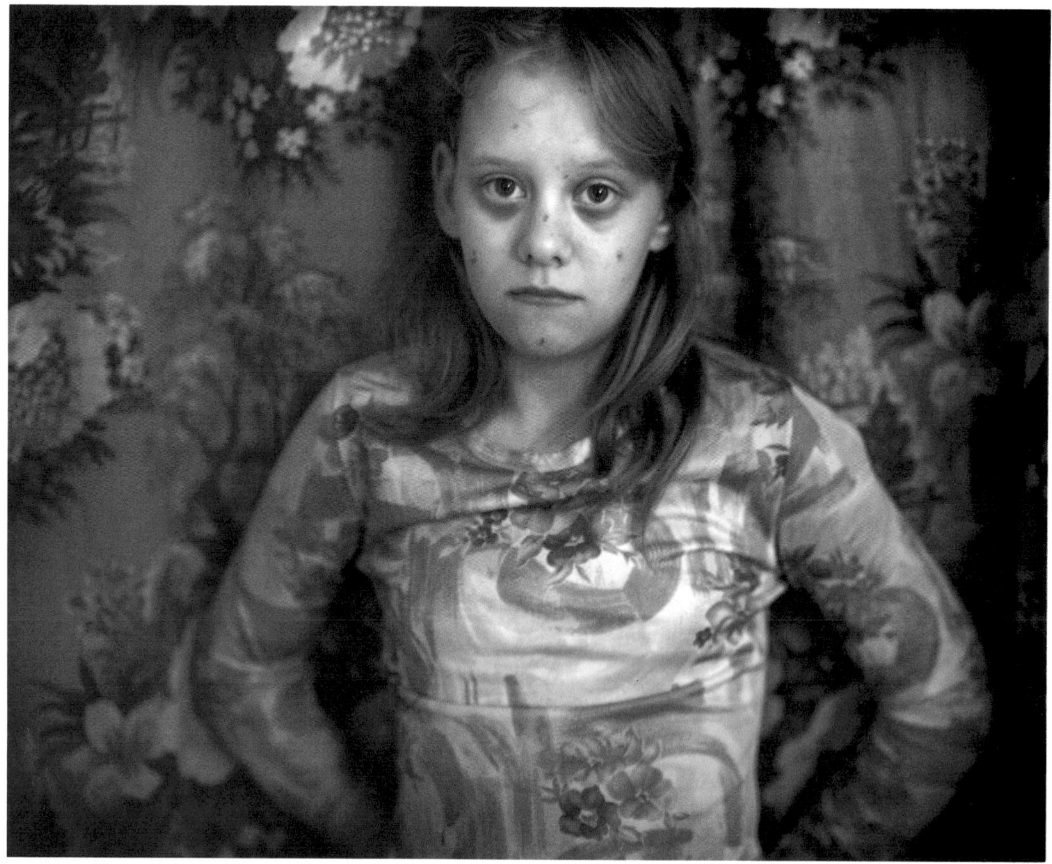

I first saw Cindy in the lunch line. She was standing alone. I called her mother that night, and she said I could photograph Cindy anytime I wanted.

I would pick up Cindy and her two little brothers after school. They fought over who got to sit up front, the two losers ending up wedged between Emmett and Jessie in their car seats in back. They loved to just drive around in the early spring air listening to the radio. We would talk about their lives. Often no pictures were taken and it would be late when I took them home. Most times the house would be dark.

Their yard was nothing but dirt, and it was mud that gray Easter when I drove out there. Rounding the bend, I stopped in the road. Dancing above the slush, weaving along the path to the outhouse, festooning the bare branches of the surviving bushes and spiraling through the car bodies, were hundreds of Cindy's painstakingly decorated paper flowers.

I grew to love those three children in that deficient, mournful way that one loves those beyond reach. As their lives began to unravel, I found them living in the back of a car parked outside an uncle's cabin. Then they were gone.

Several months ago the mother's boyfriend told me that Cindy had "gotten herself a baby." He had a photograph of her holding her baby and pregnant again.

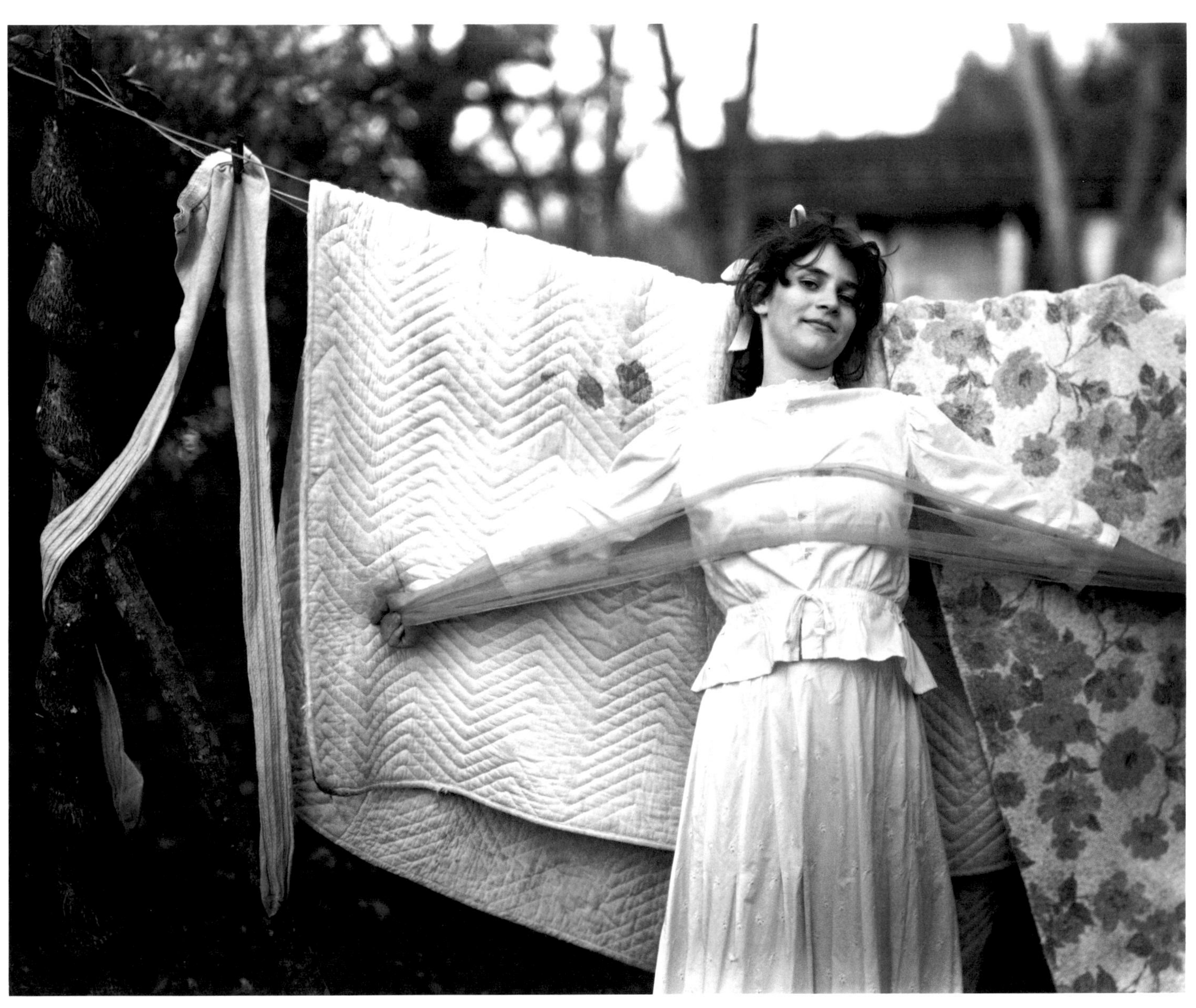

As in all transformations, there is an element of sadness. Something very familiar, very comforting is being left behind for the unknown, which beckons her, siren-like and irresistible. She is, as Rilke once observed, seated before her own heart's curtain. It allows only the tiniest peek.

Intolerable, the waiting and the melancholy. All changes, even the most longed for, must have their melancholy.

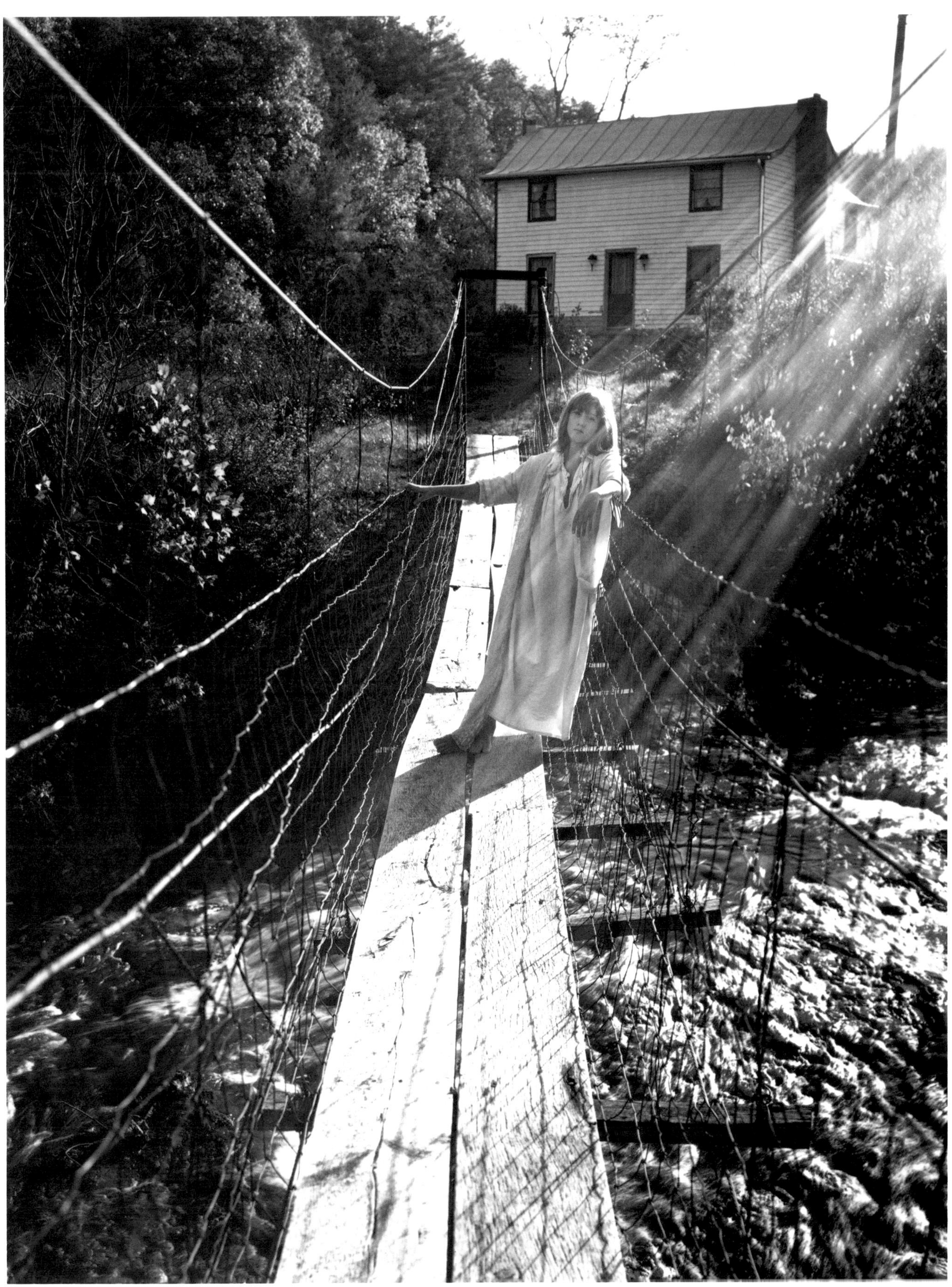

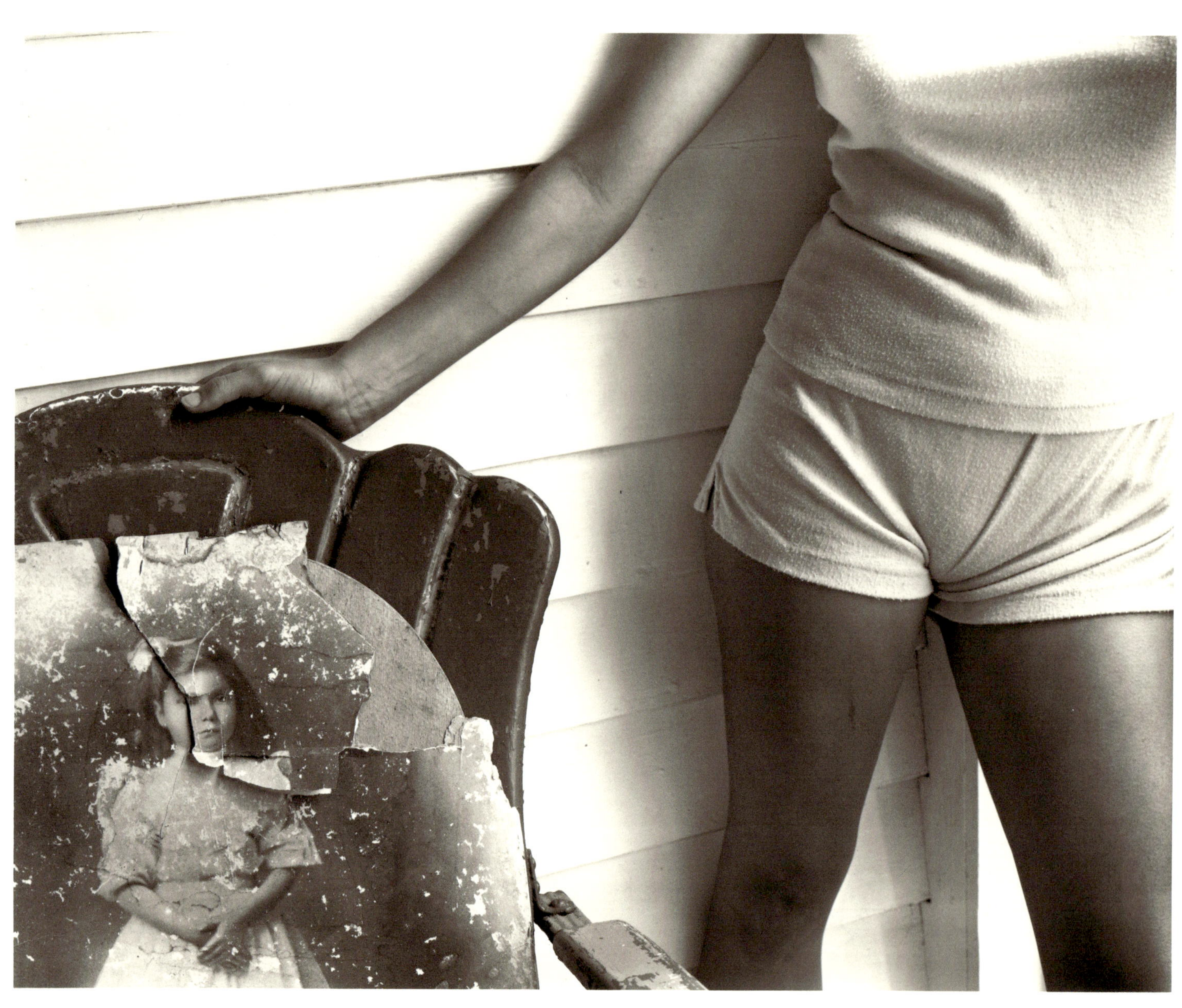

Sherry and Sherry's grandmother, both at twelve years old.

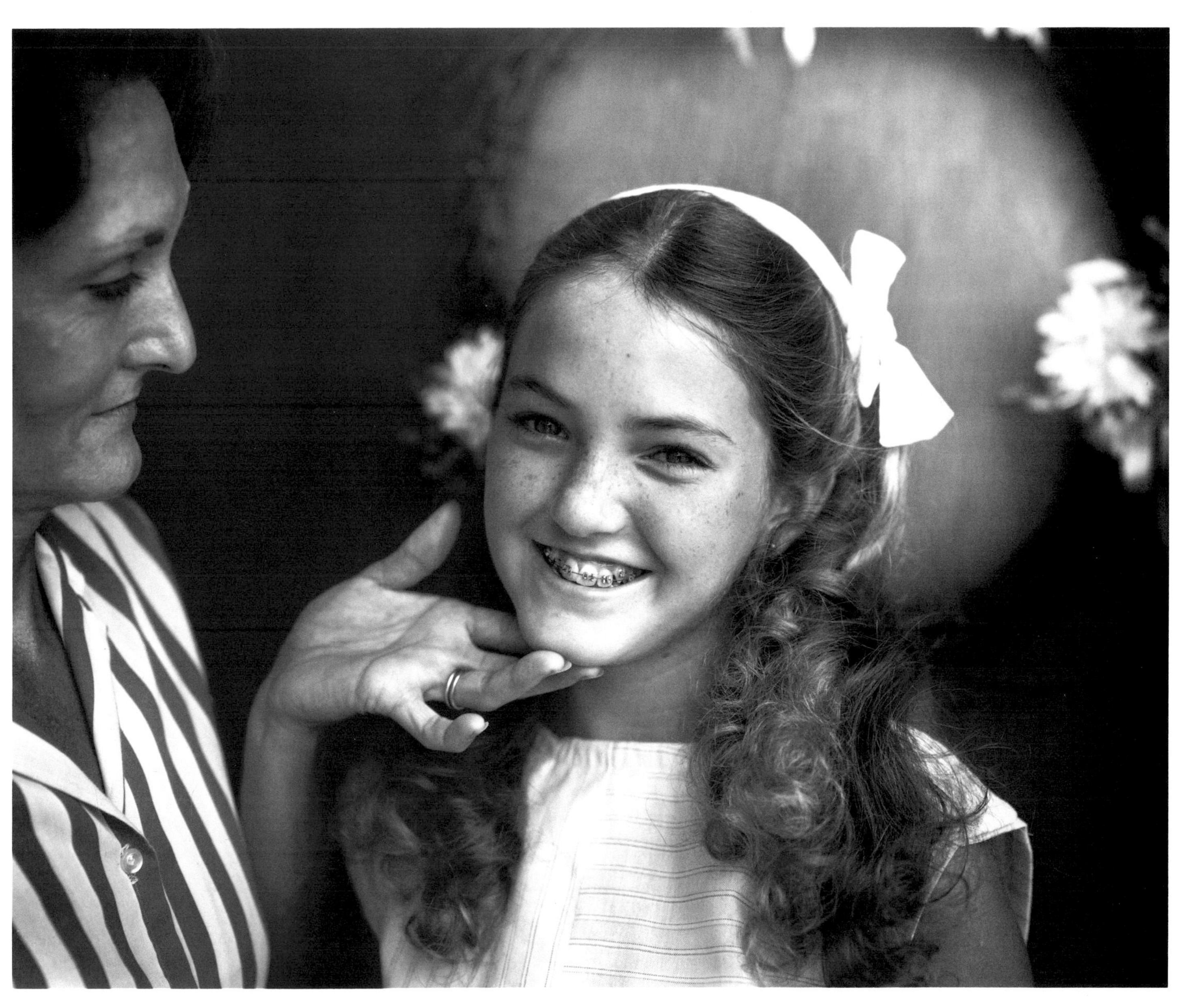

Pre-teen Miss Rockbridge gets braces.

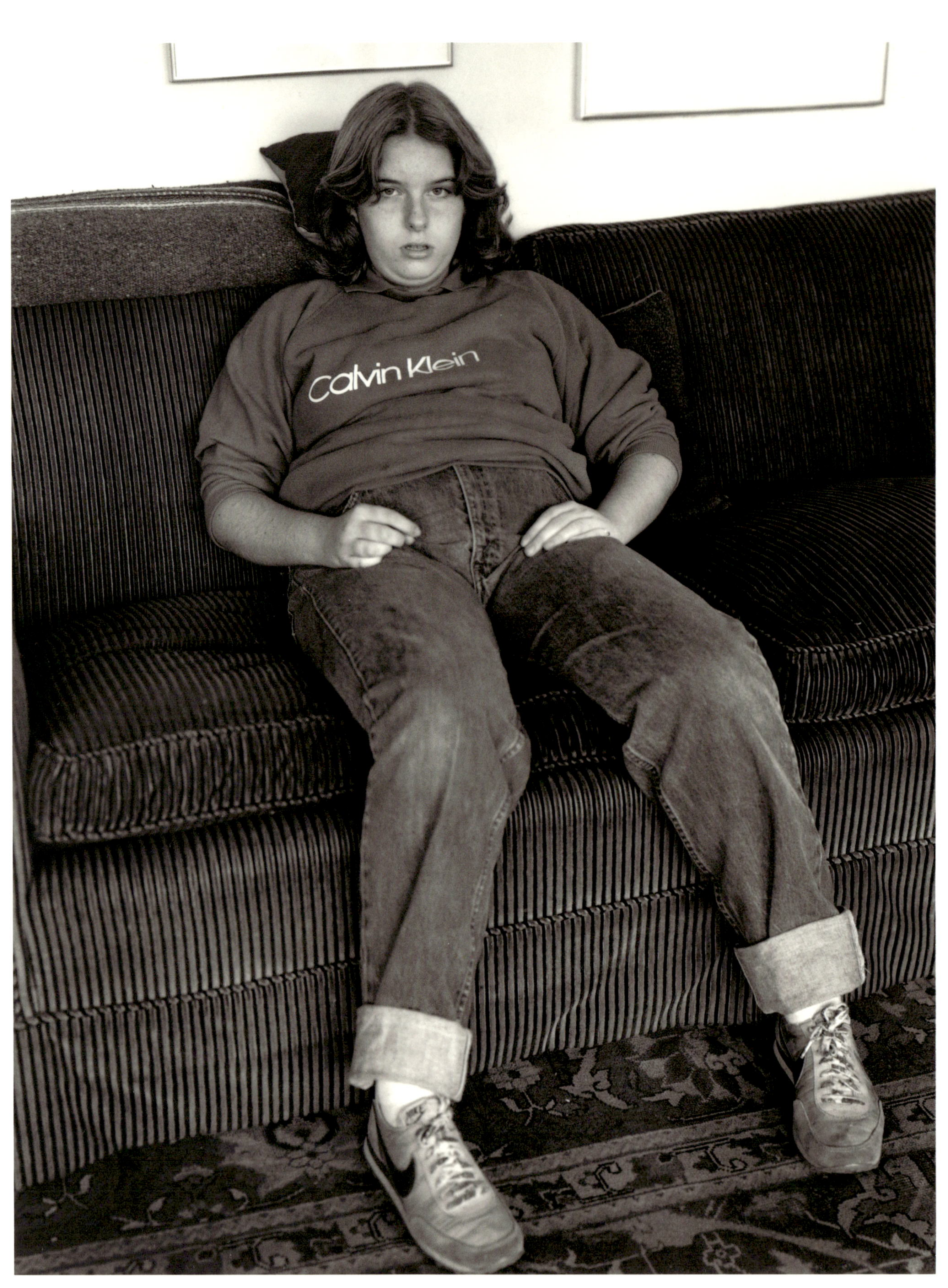
Calvin Klein

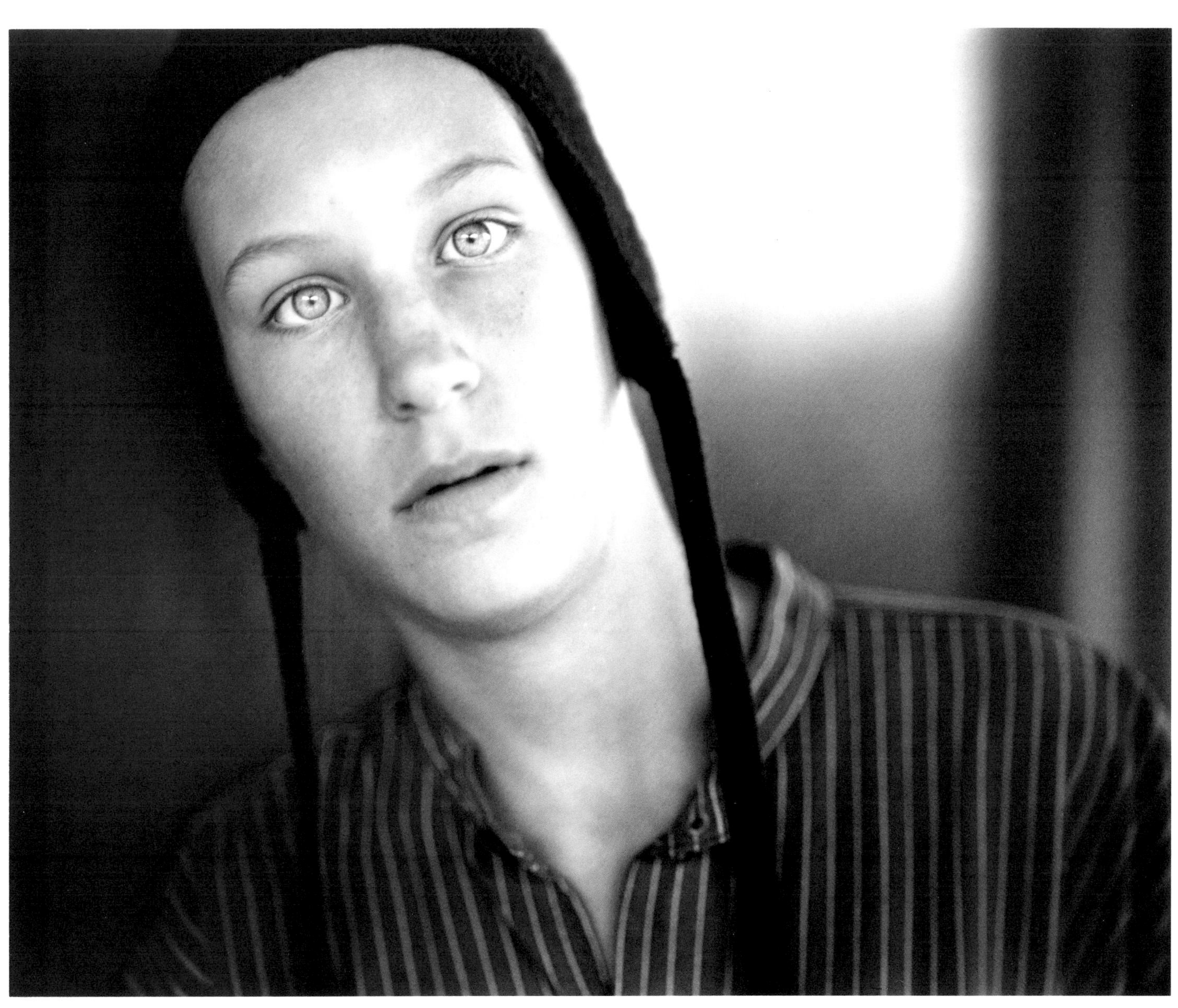

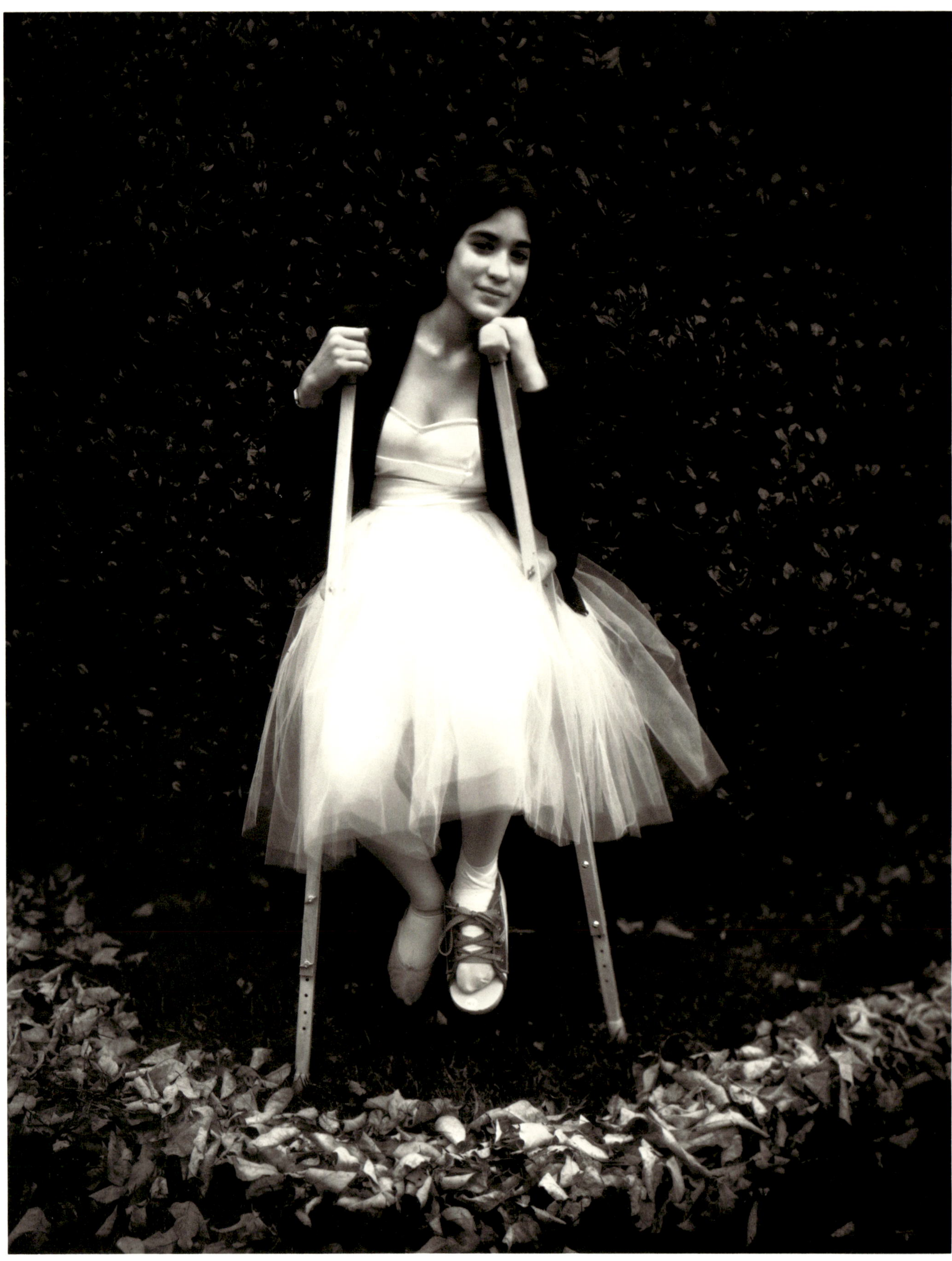

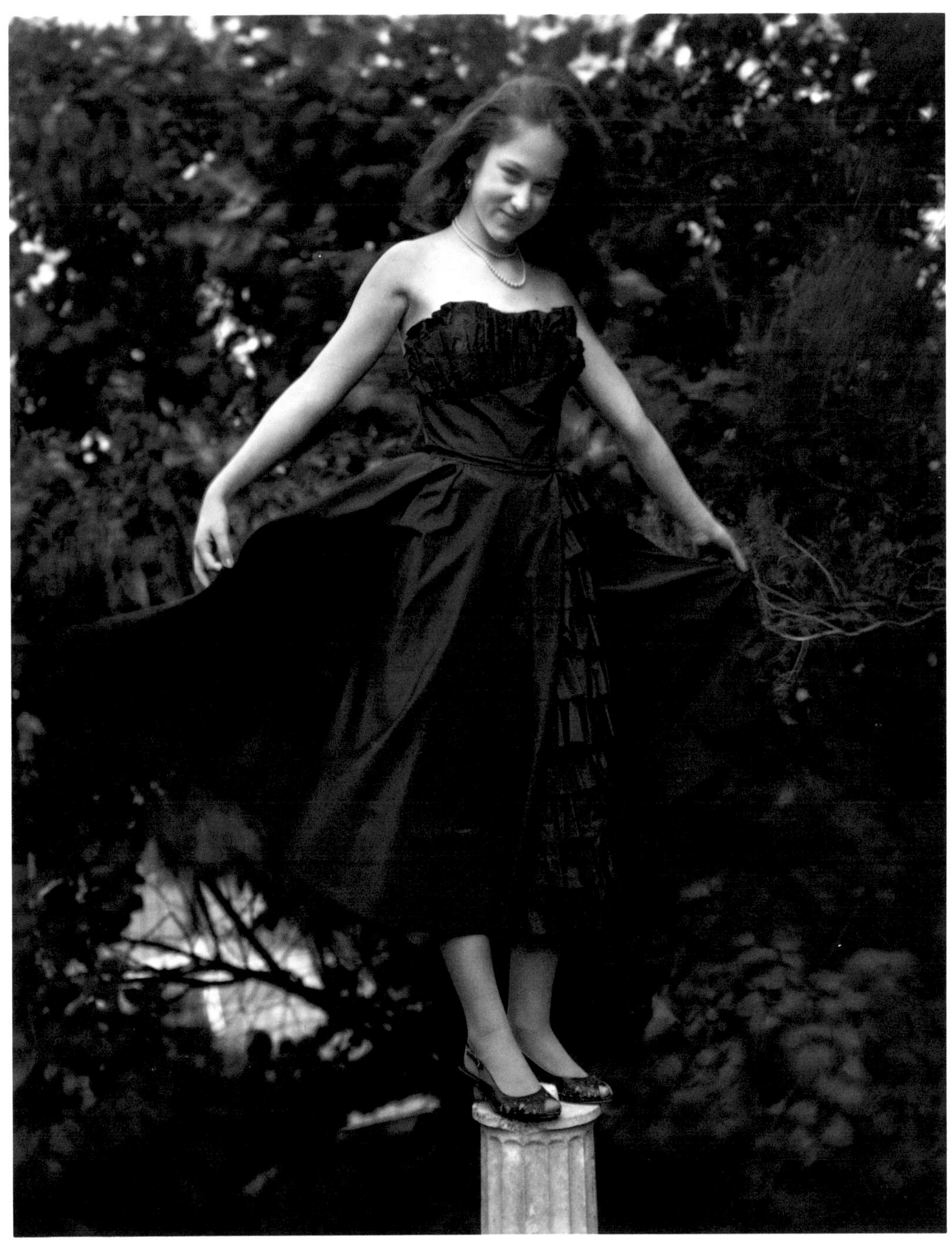

Wings spread, tentative, she is grounded still, rehearsing for the first flight. Her mother took the bird-bath off the pedestal, boosted her up, and stood beaming as she unfolded. No doubt from the height of the pedestal she seemed small to her daughter, like a chrysalis, the dry shell, once nurturing, now left behind.

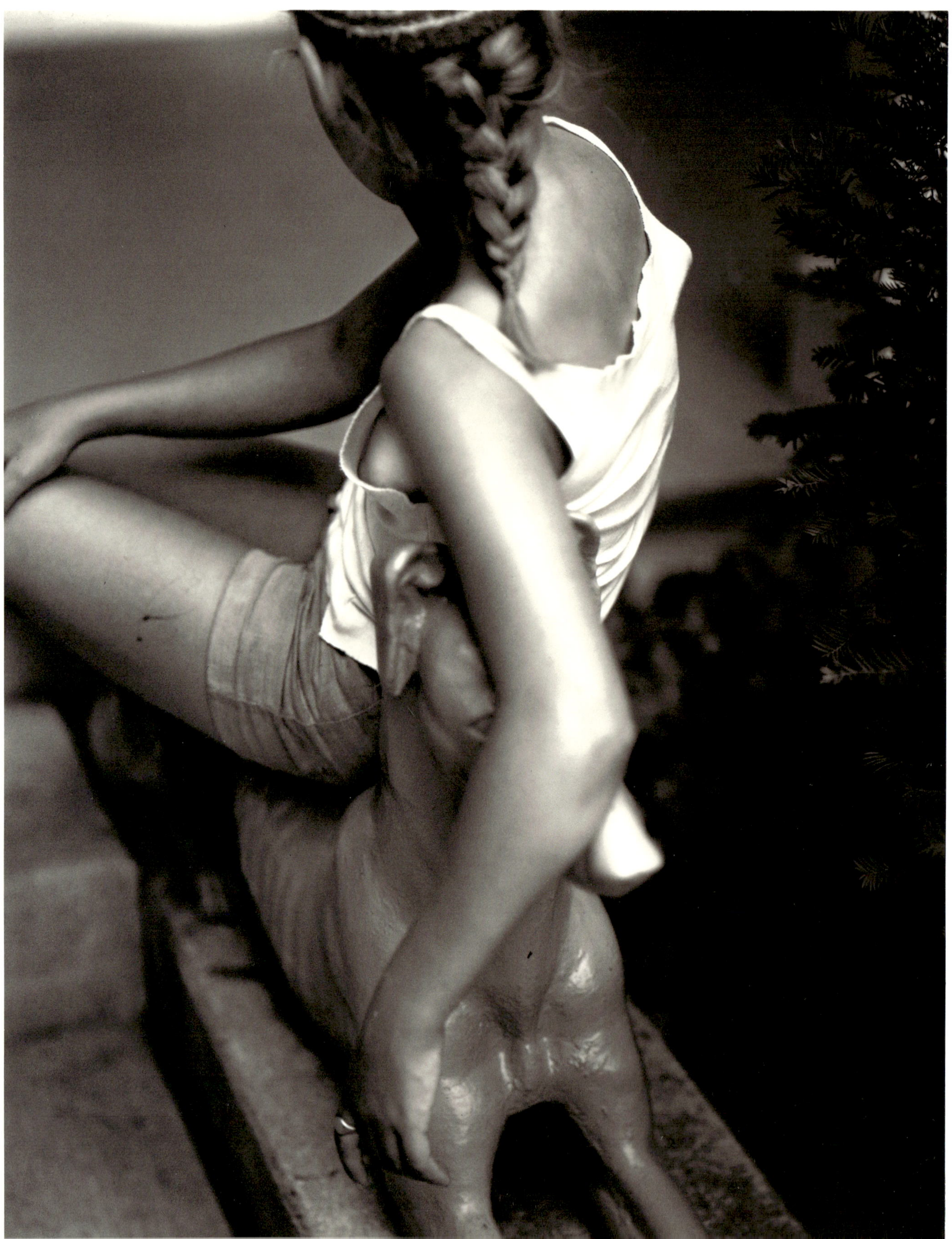

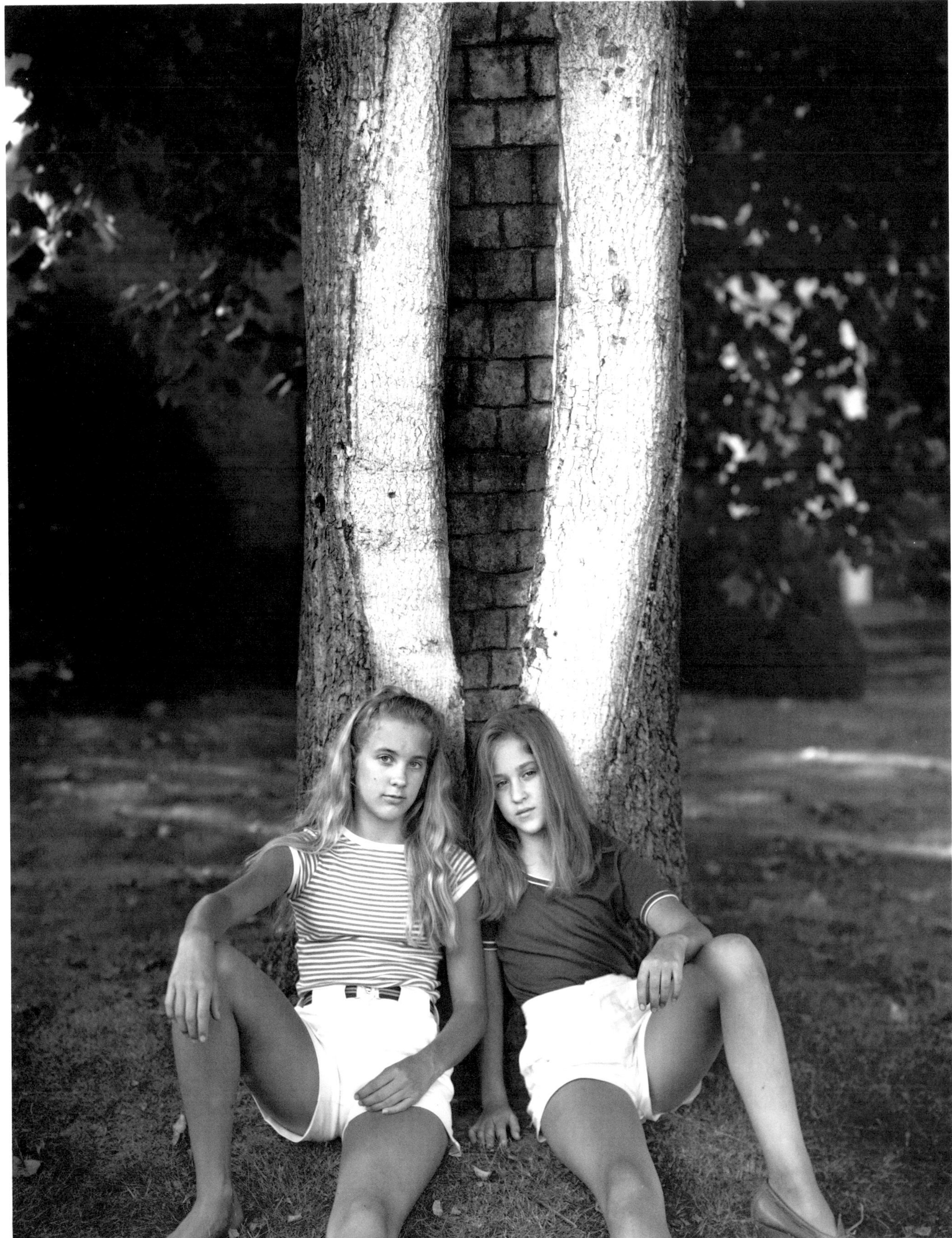

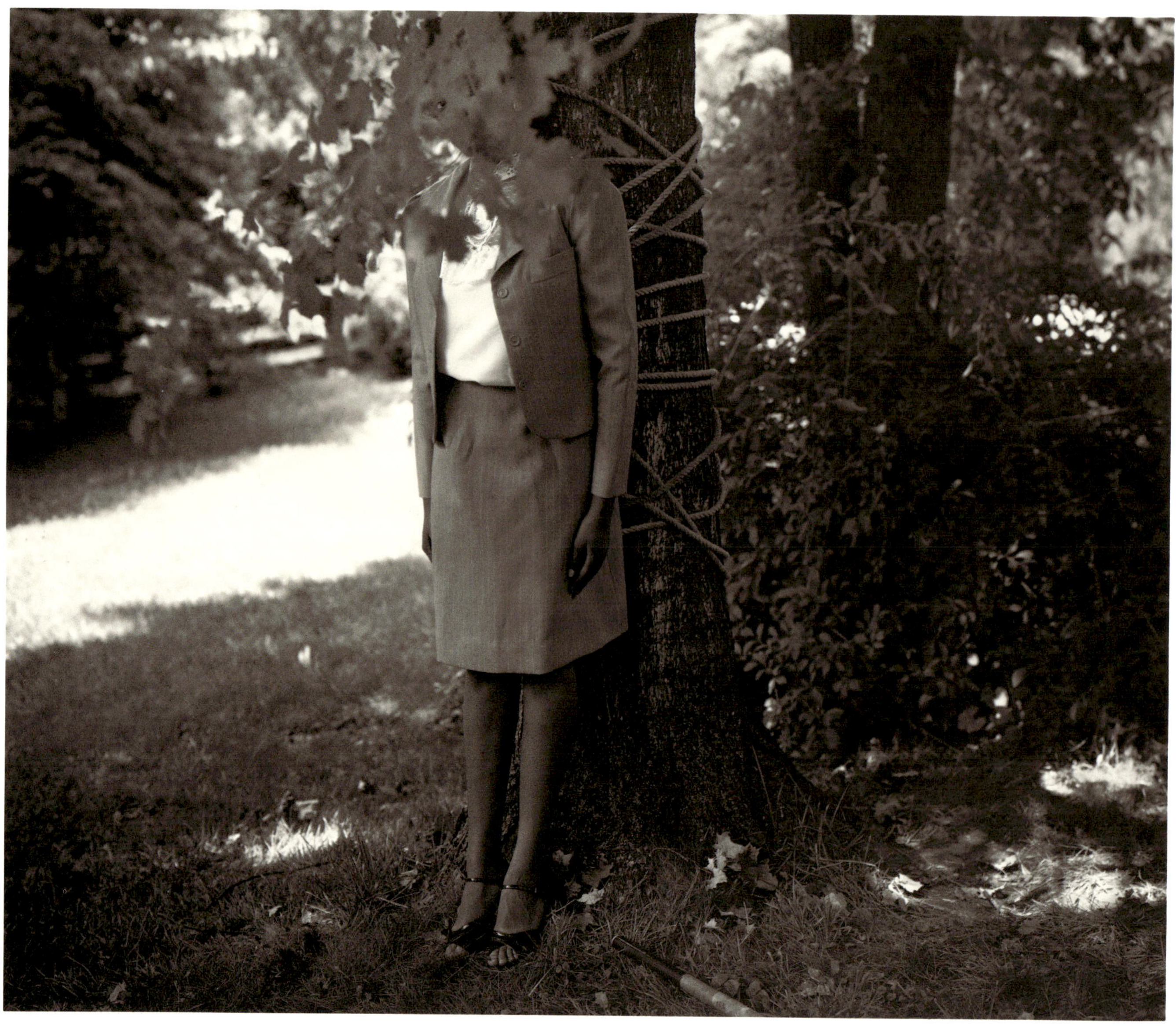

I saw her eye there, peeking at me through a tiny chink in the foliage—cautious, the only sign of a child's curiosity. She had come out of her apartment dressed as if she were on her way to a job interview. I was confounded by her reserve and composure. I couldn't imagine what picture I would take midday, midsummer, of this girl more woman than I.

It had been there for six months, around the corner on White Street, the bound tree. We did not speak. She stood absolutely still, only the veiled eye shifting in the still heat.

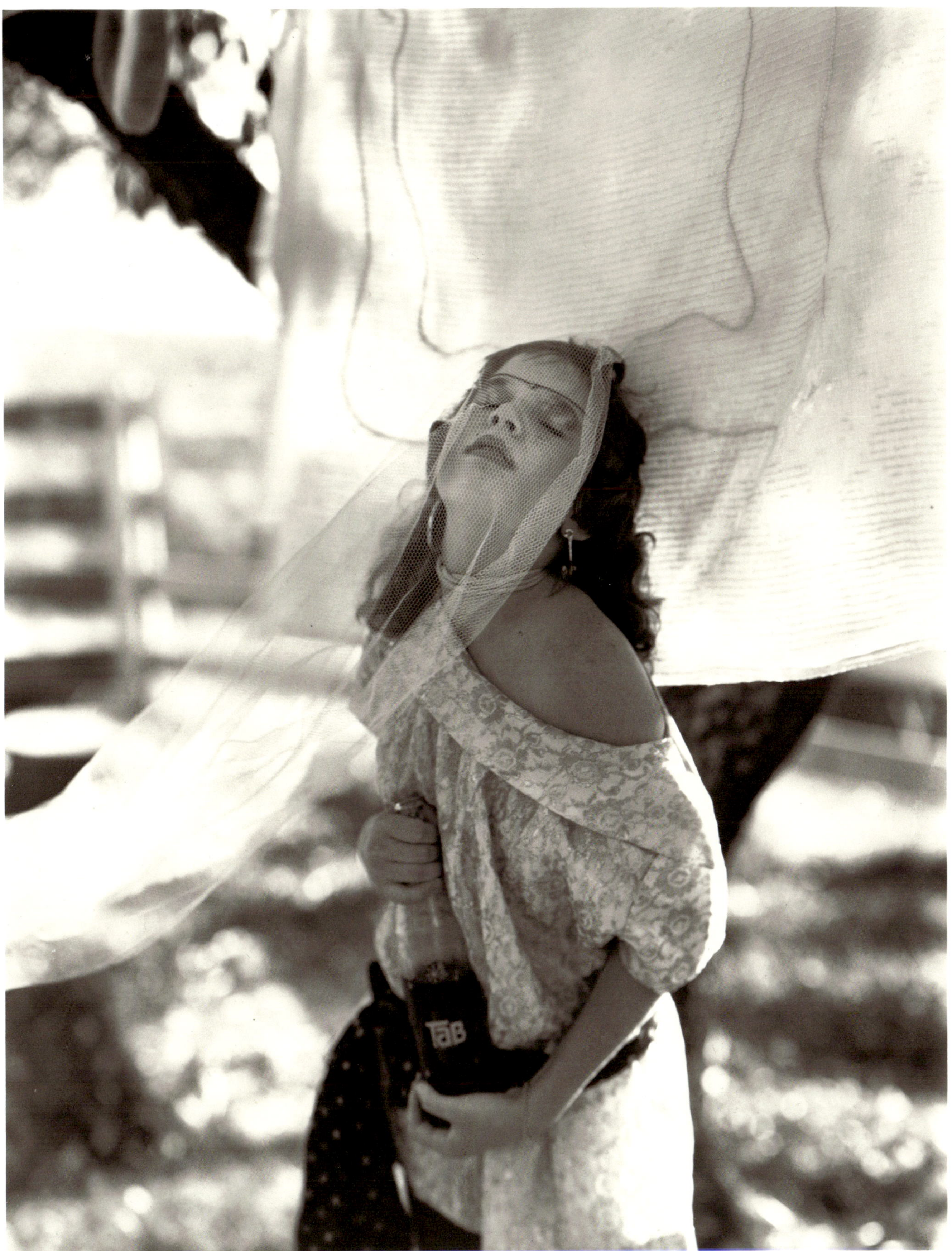
TaB

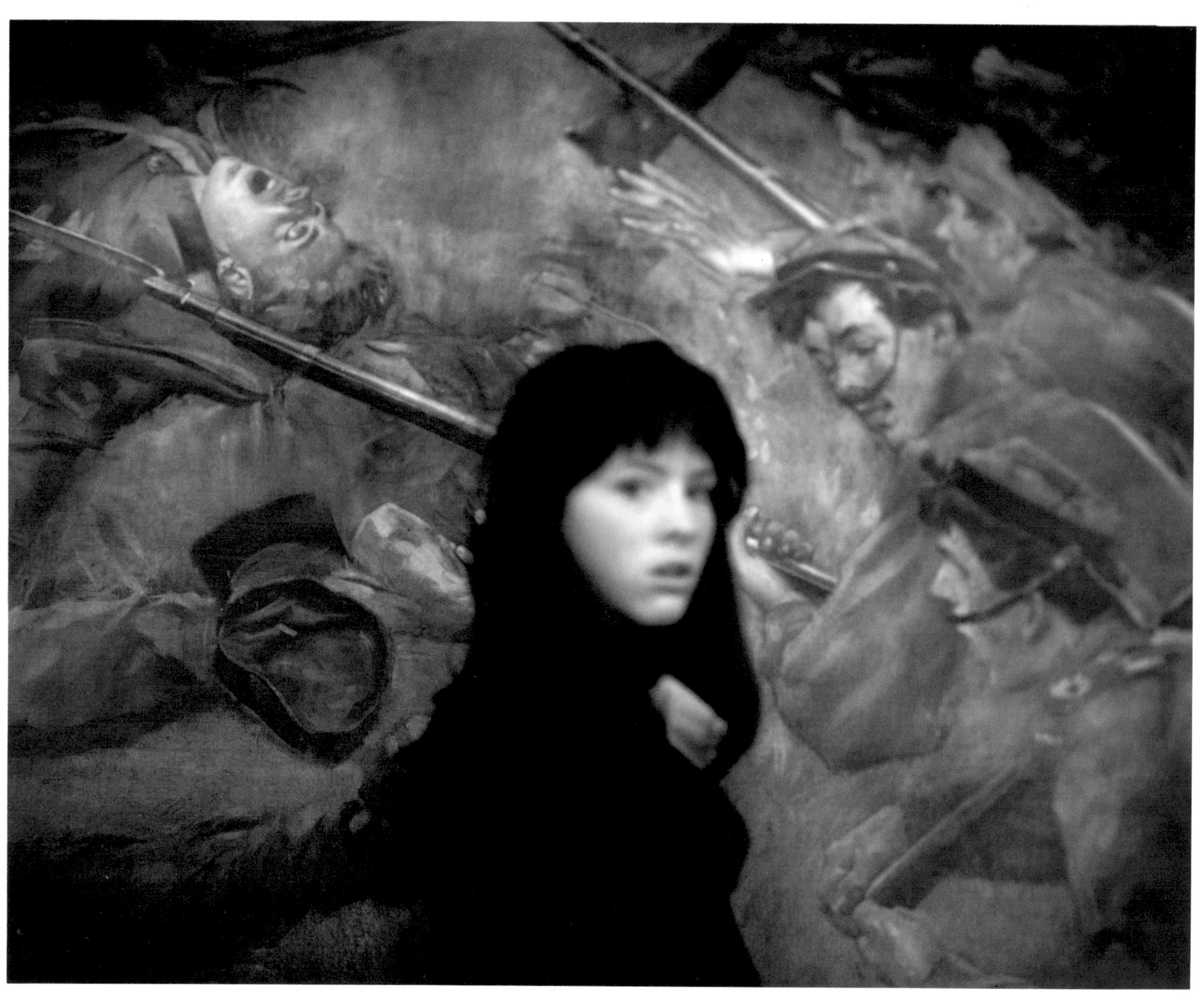

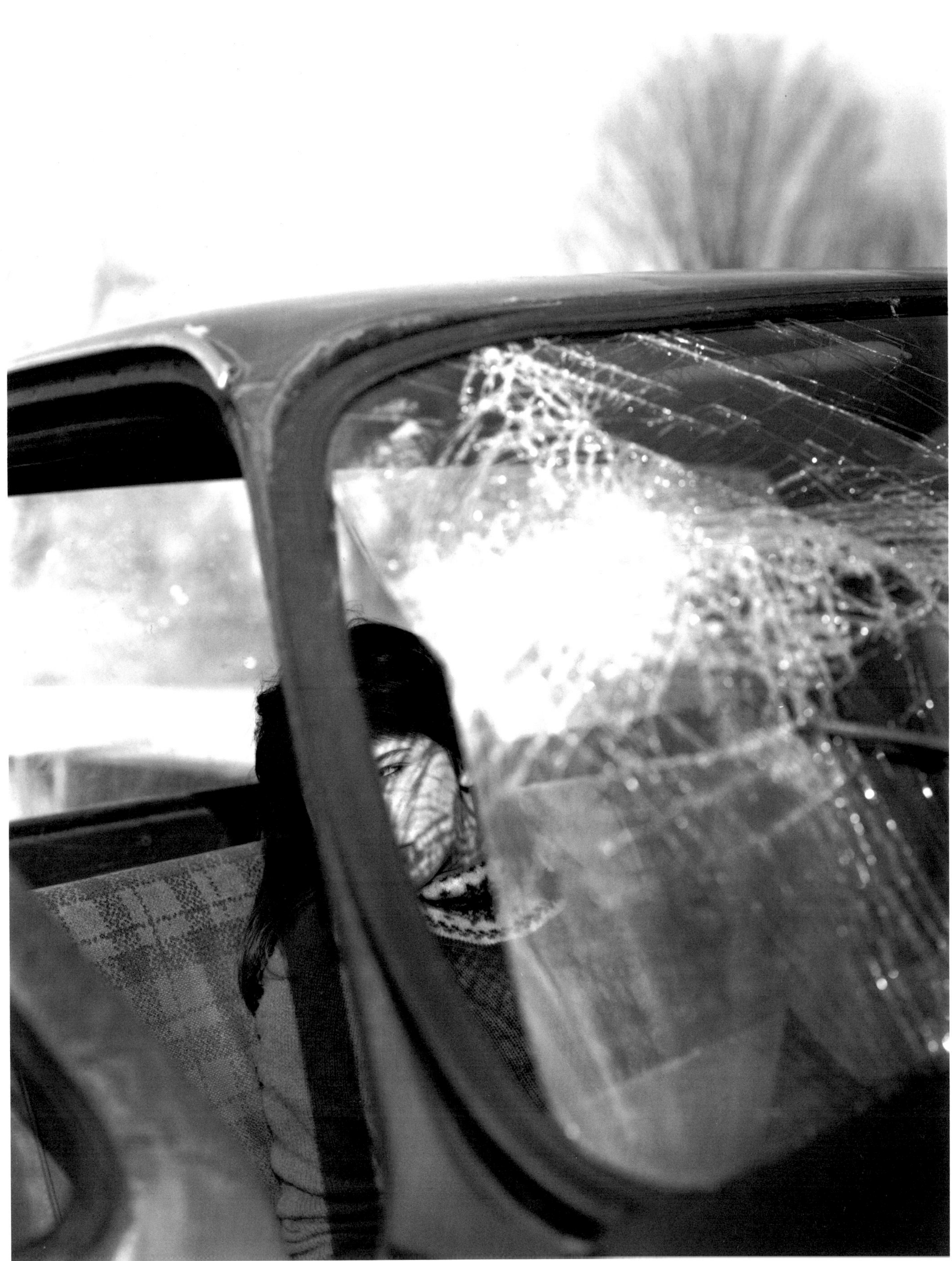

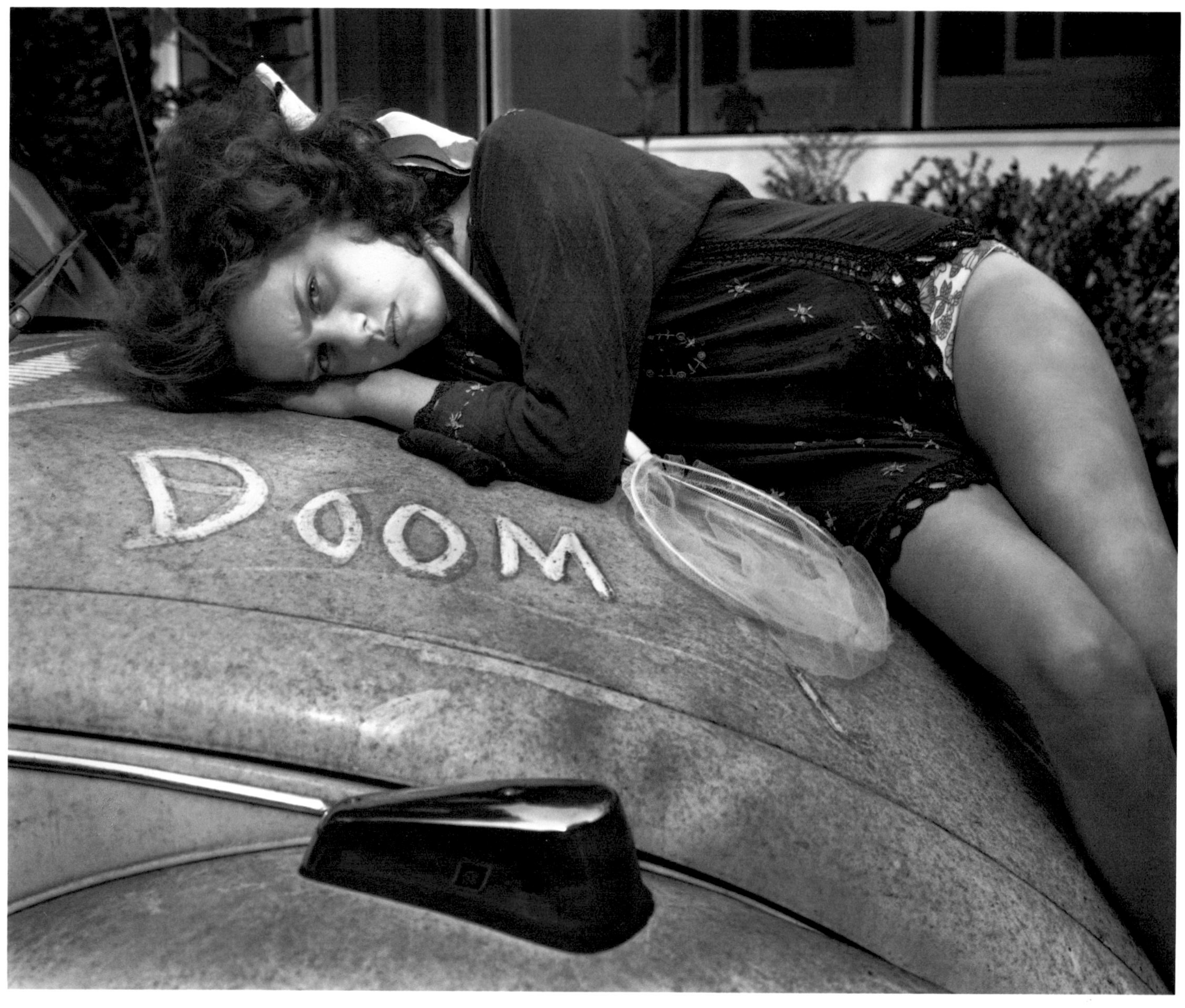

Showing me how her mother's boyfriend pretended
to hang himself out in the back yard.

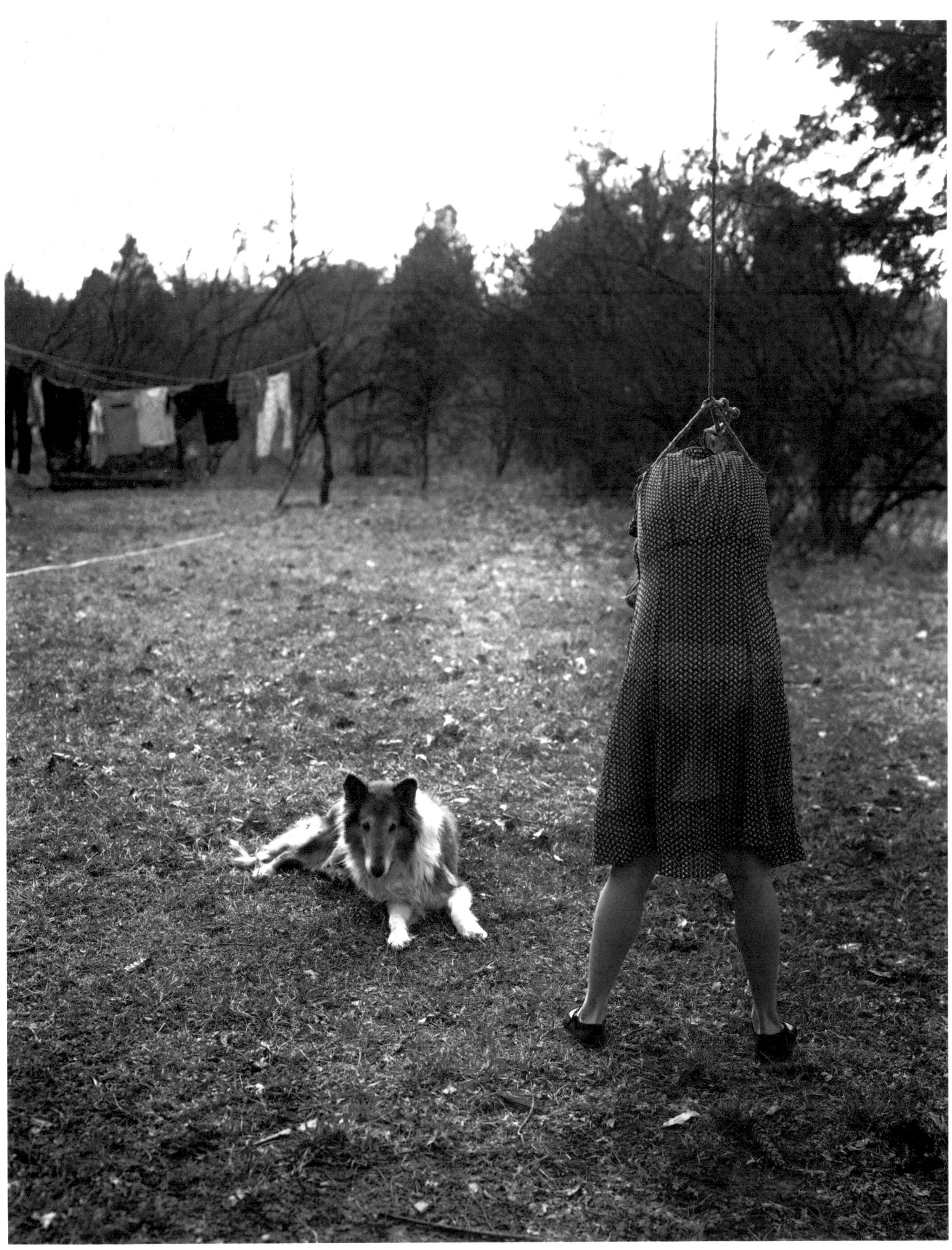

In the early fall, I drank coffee with several generations of the Conner family, the close air of their kitchen settling across my shoulders like a shawl. I explained what I was doing and, as so often happened, their initial suspicion gave way gradually to caution and then to curiosity and a guarded acceptance. They agreed that I could photograph Kelly.

At dawn on the first day of hunting season they called when the deer were beheaded and hung. As I set up the camera, Kelly appeared, buttoned up, accompanied by her mother, her aunt and uncle, her grandparents, cousins, and a few other family members. Arrayed behind me, they remained watchful and intent.

As I pulled her jacket back, to separate her white-shirted figure from the darkness of the shed, I thought I might have heard a murmur. After a few minutes I relaxed enough to identify the prevalence of the V shapes in the scene and without thinking I asked Kelly to spread her legs. This time the murmur was audible, but I could see that the picture was complete.

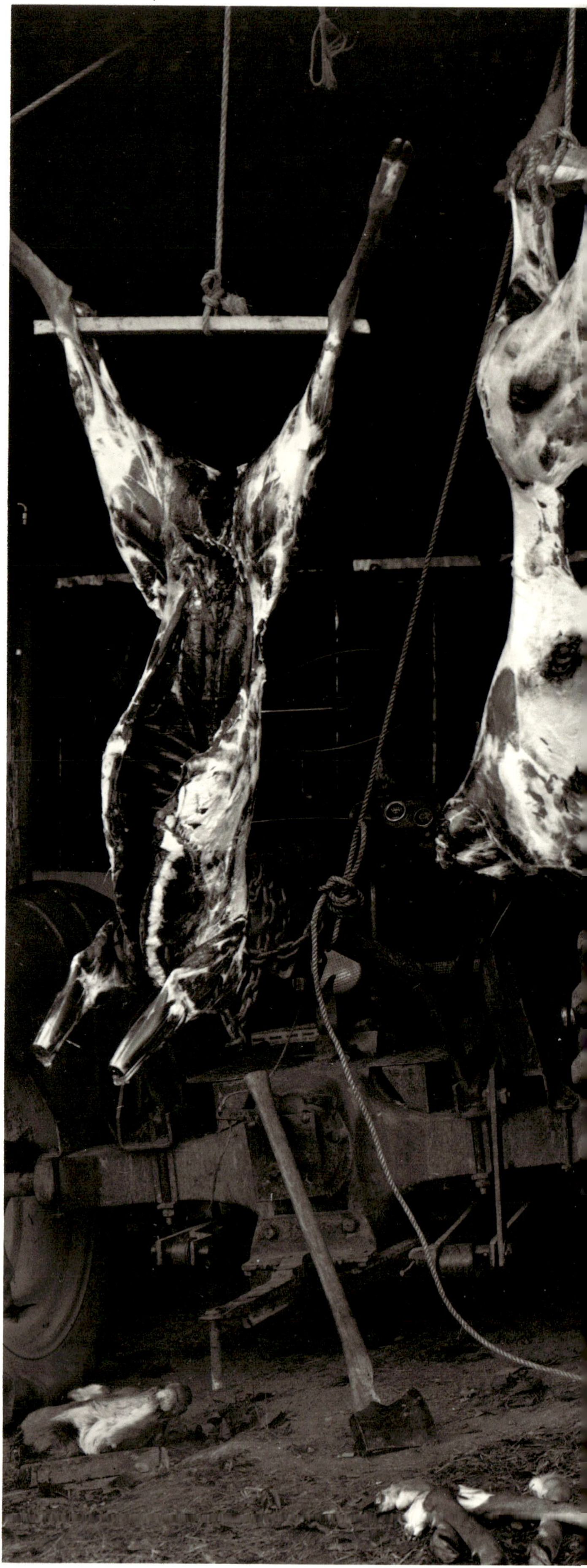

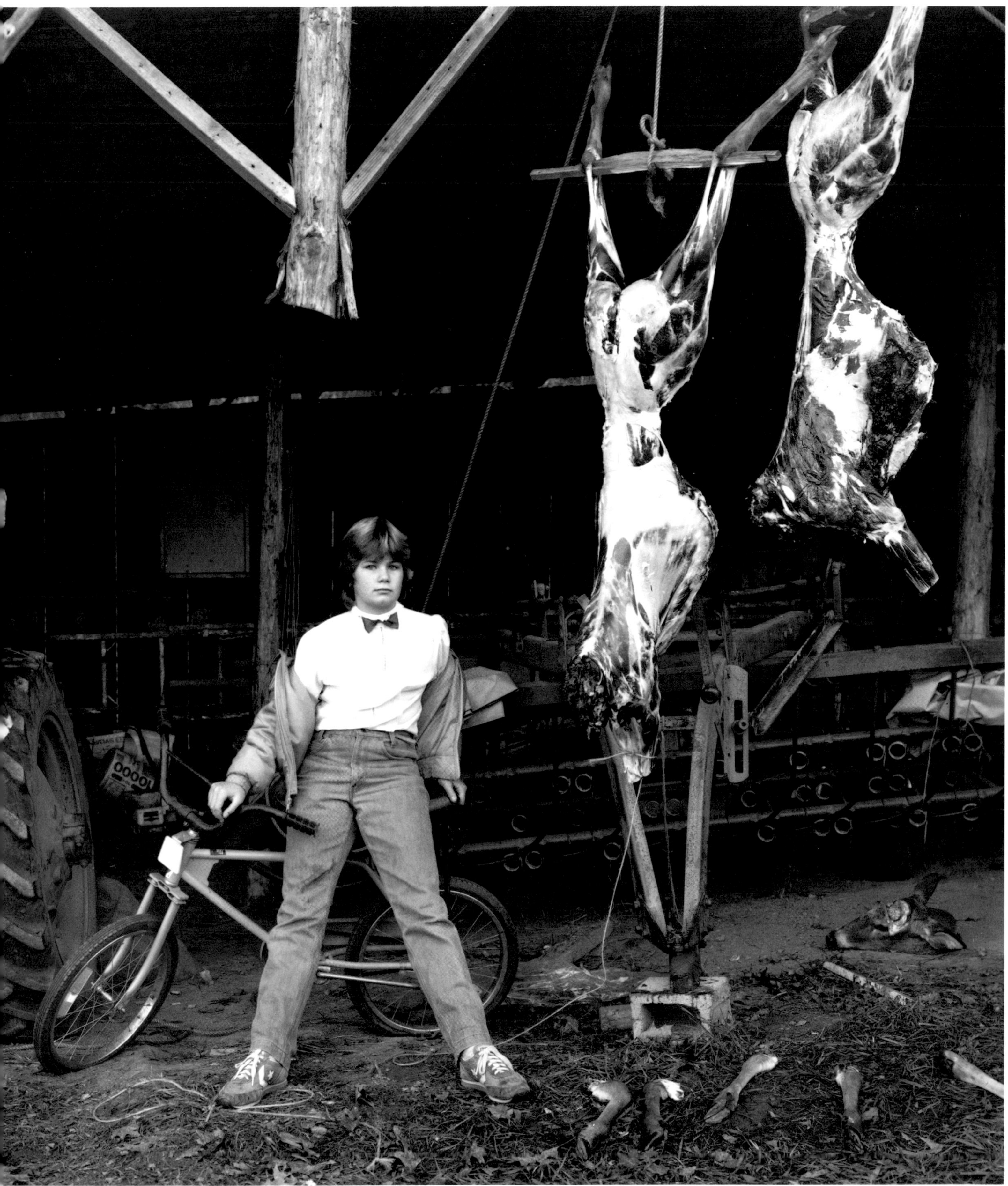

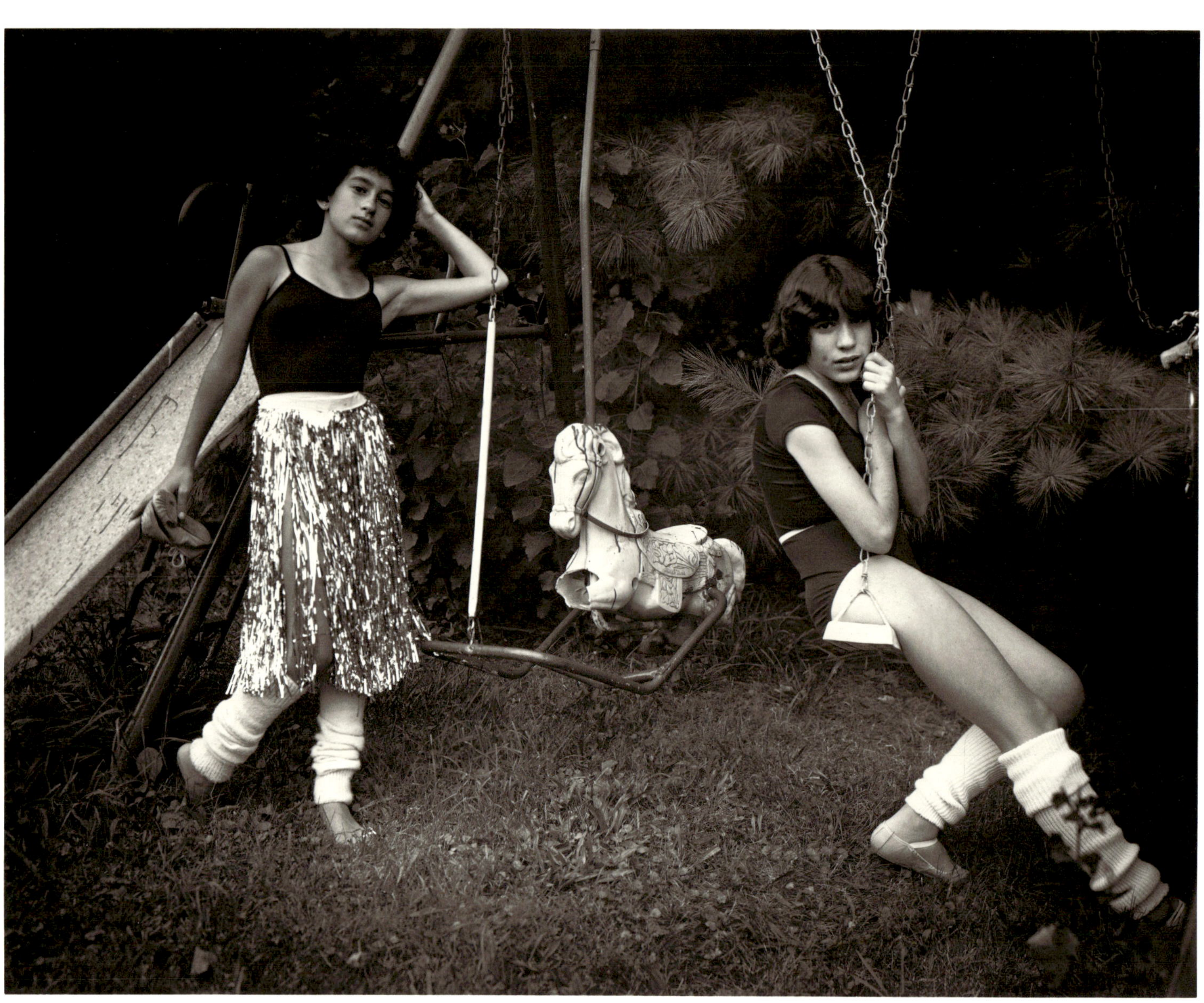

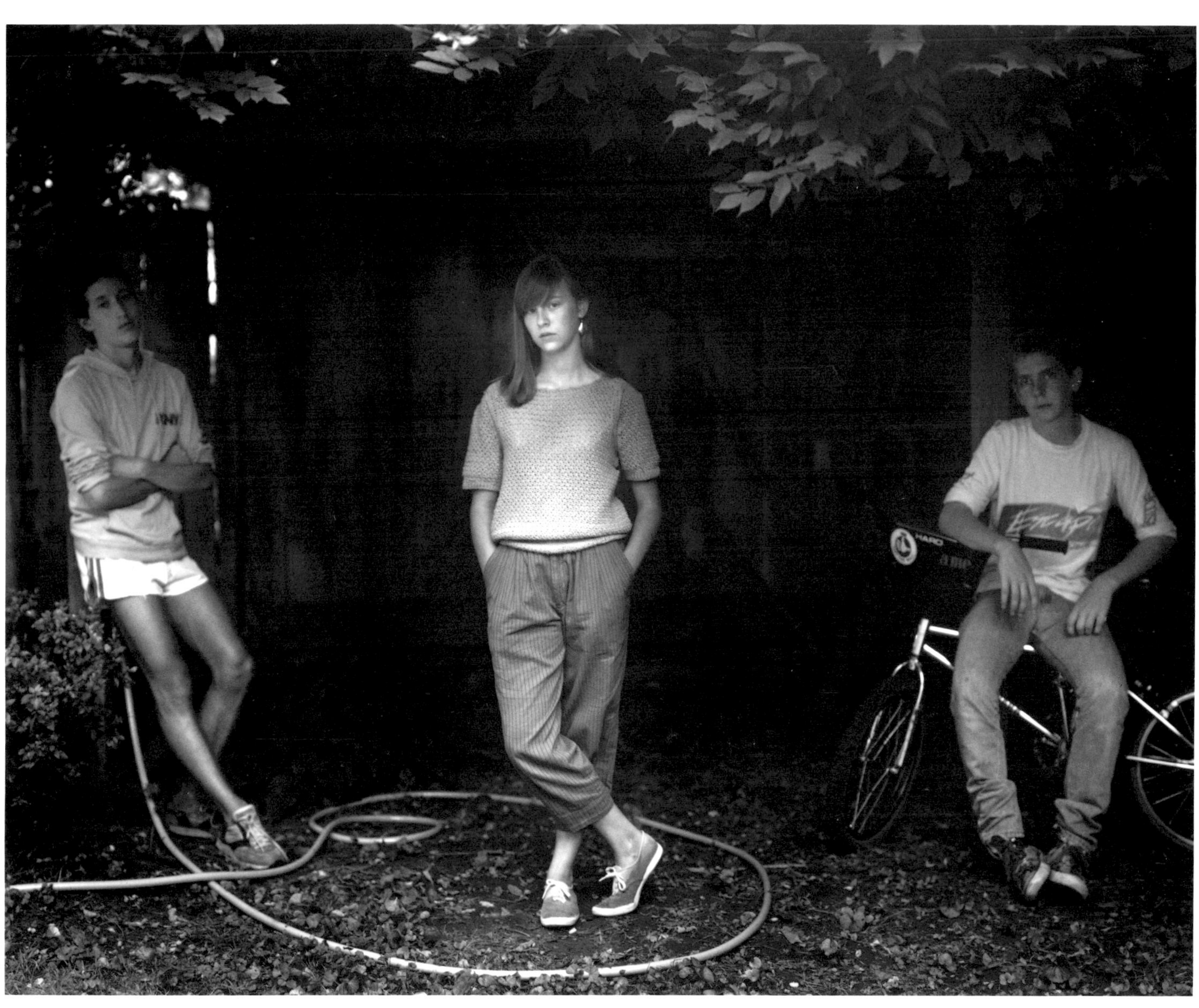

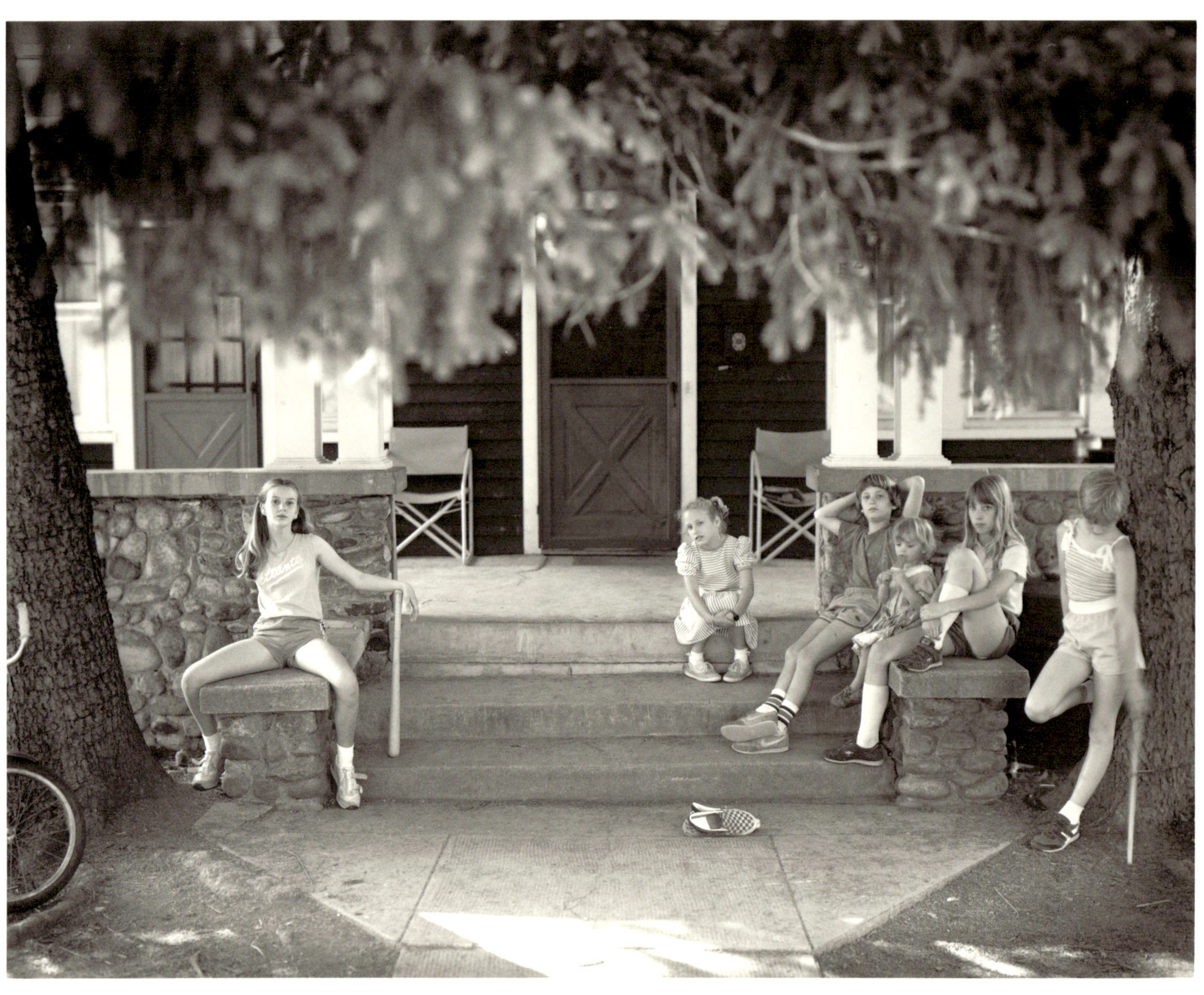

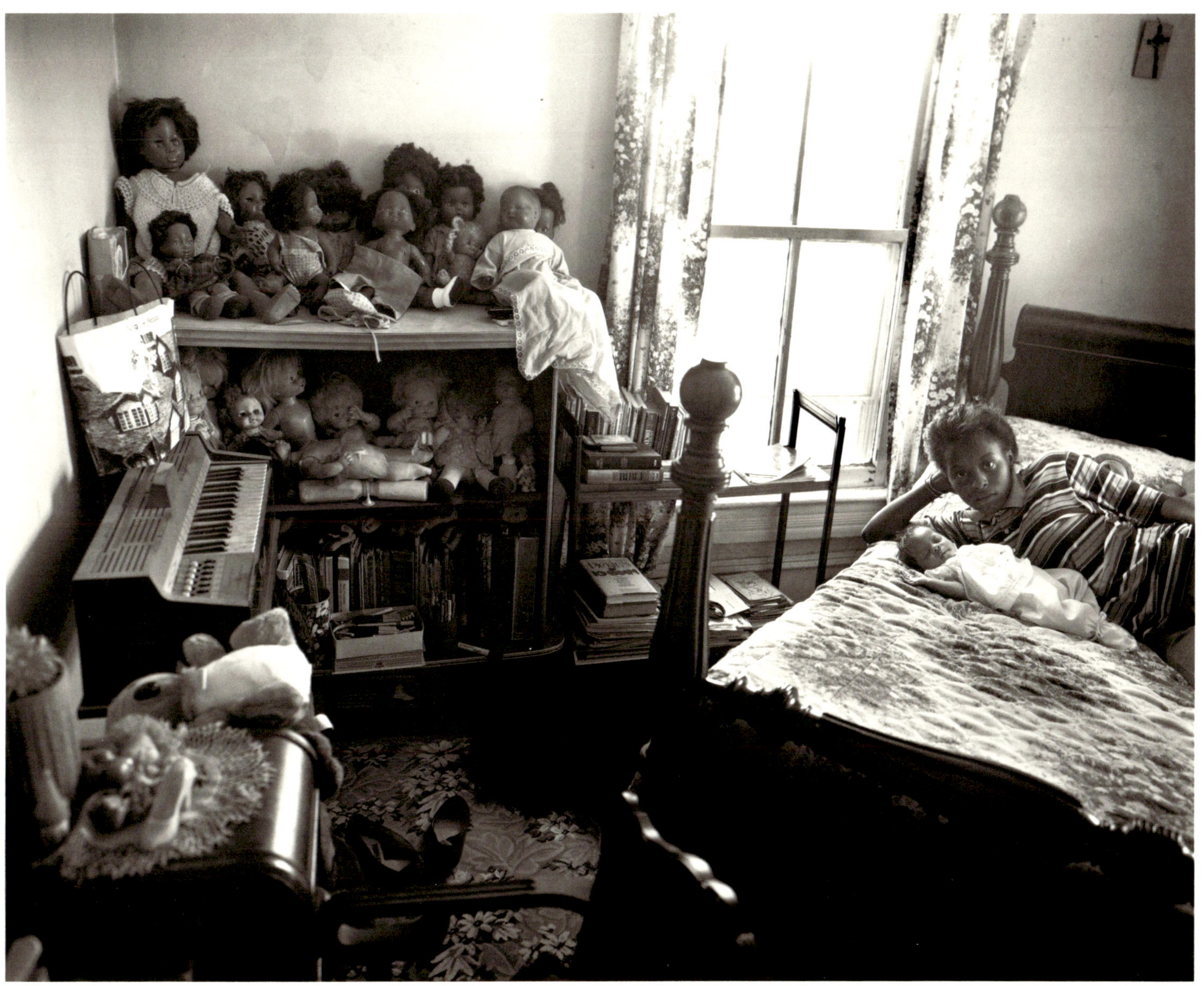

Theresa got pregnant when she was eleven. She arranged to have an abortion but somebody from an agency of the Catholic church visited her and asked her first to watch a few movies about abortion. Theresa decided to have the baby. I asked her if the people who showed her the movies had ever been back in touch with her now that she is a mother, and she said no but that it was O.K. She and her great-grandmother, who is legally blind, raise the baby in a house full of glass figurines.

Once we were driving along and my hair was wafting up toward the open sun-roof. She said that she used to wish she was white and had long red hair. I gripped the steering wheel a little more tightly and waited. But, she added, now she just puts raspberry Kool-Aid on her hair to give it red highlights.

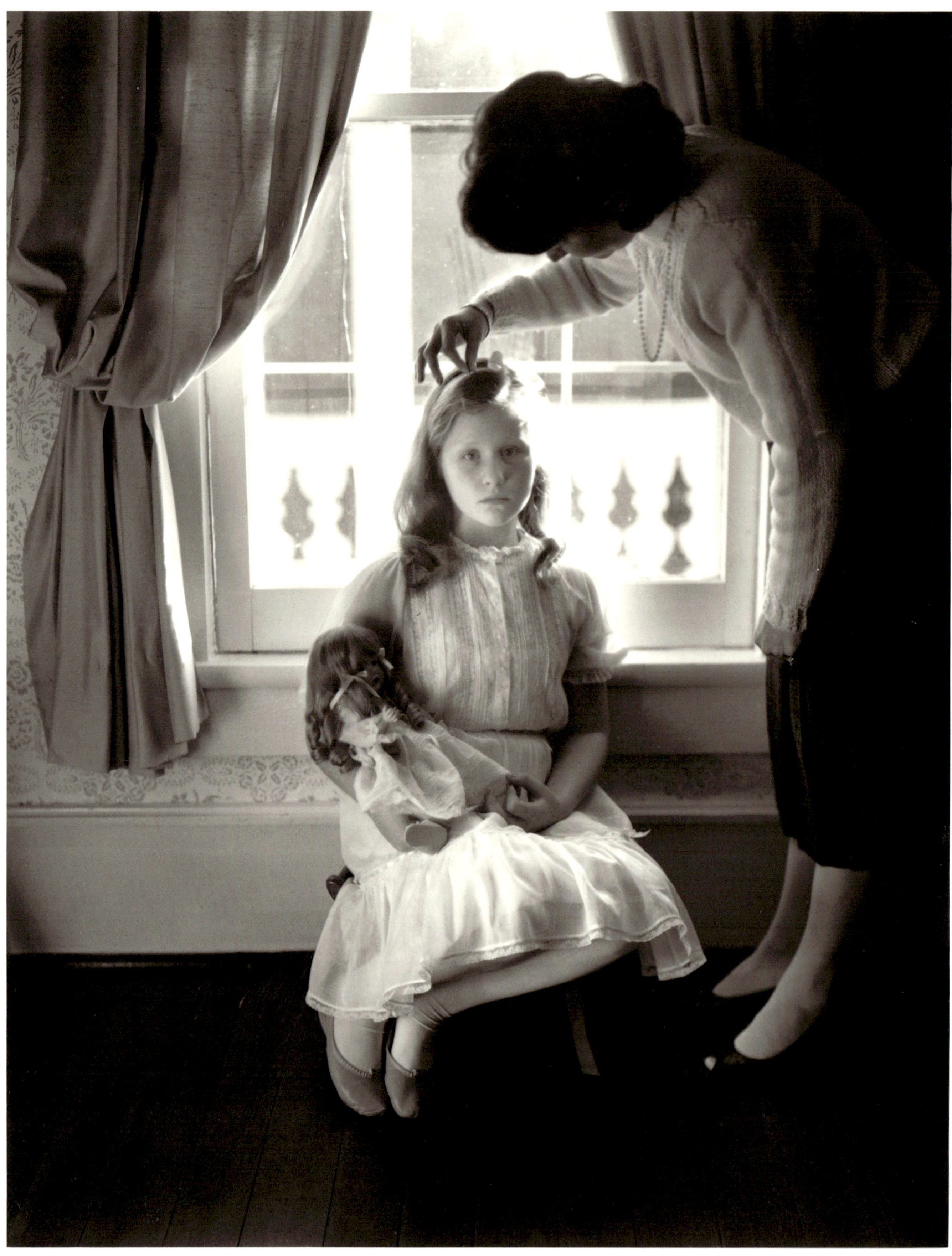

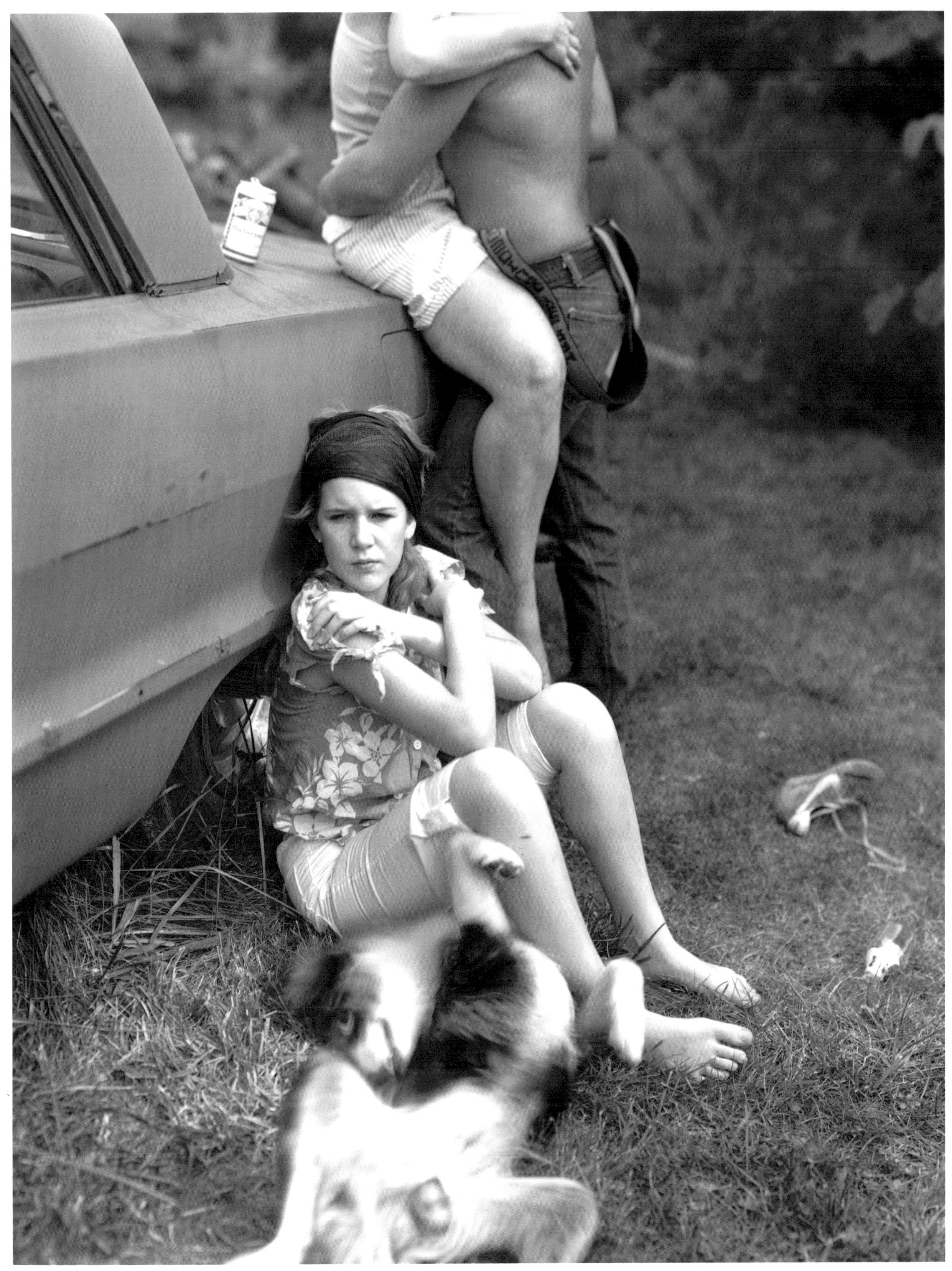

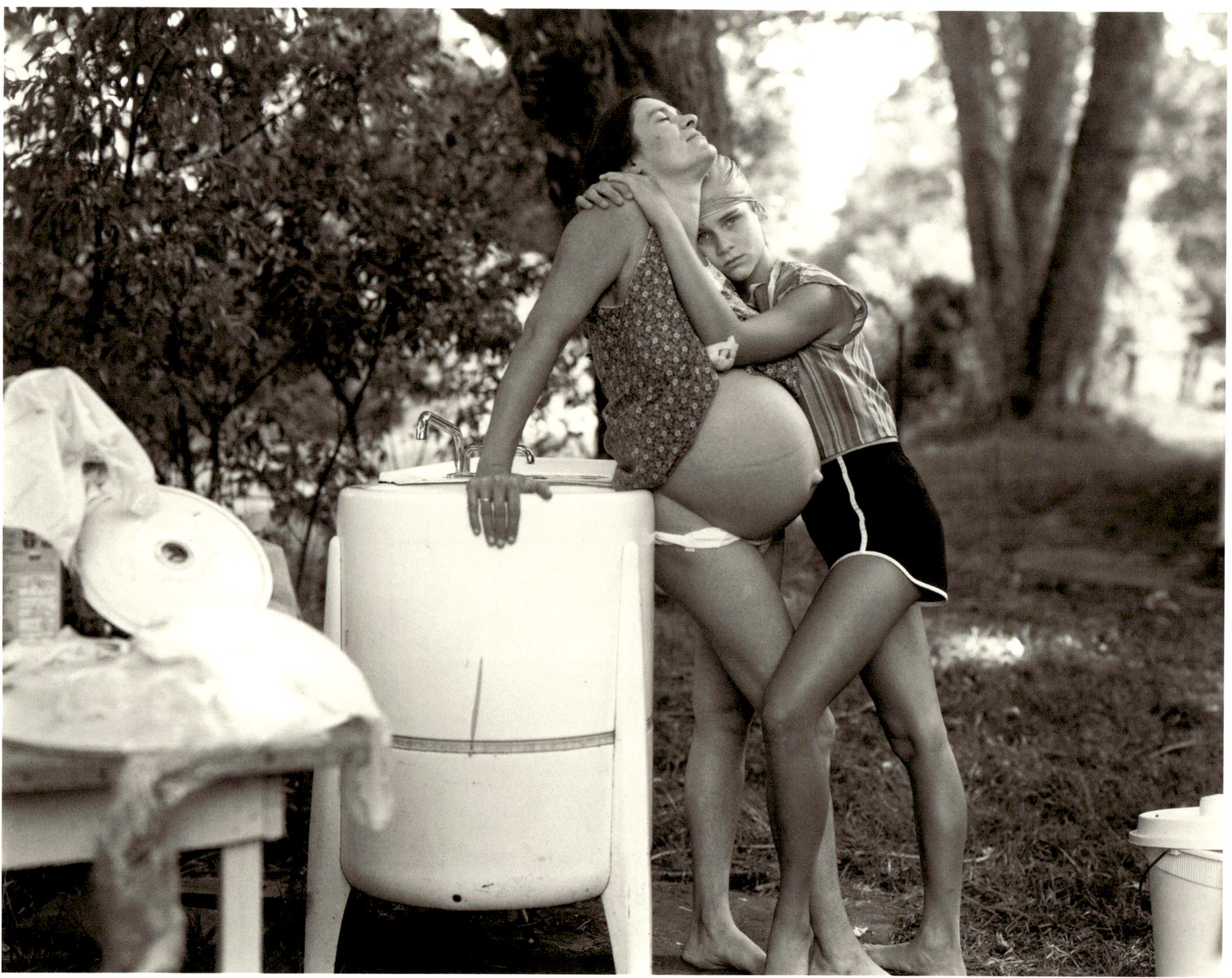

Leslie and I both were pregnant with our third children when this photograph was taken. Each with two babies already, we shared those universal feelings of resignation, ambivalence, and determination. It was late summer and the humid Virginia heat was almost unendurable. She had only six weeks to go.

I thought the kindest thing to do was to let her lie down. She did, on a mattress out in the back yard. But prone, she did not appear nearly as large as she did upright, and I said so. Somewhat indignantly she lumbered to her feet and yanked her dress up above her sticky belly and said, with an edge of defiance: "*There. Take that then.*"

Laughing, her daughter Jenny came over to her, and we took the picture.

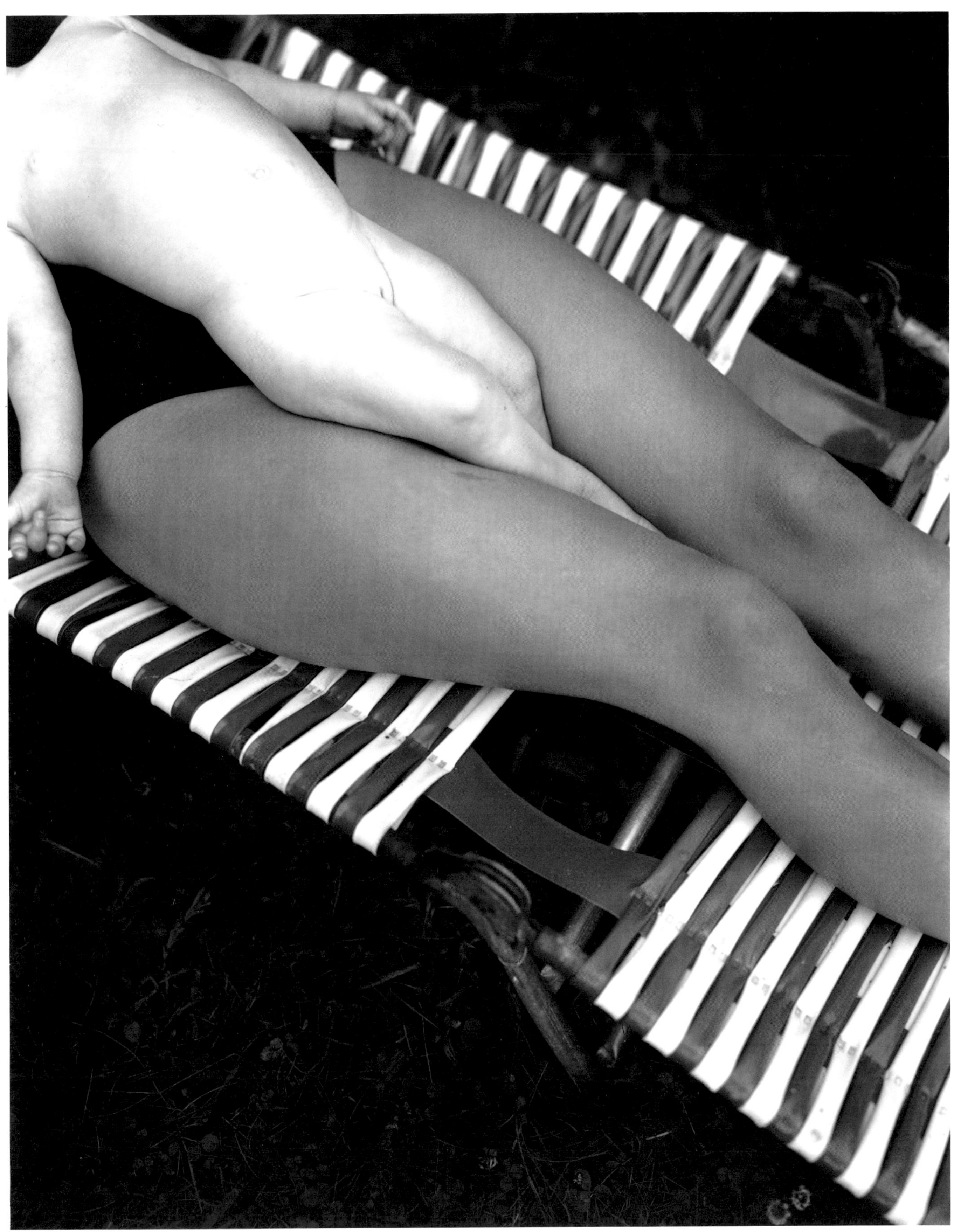

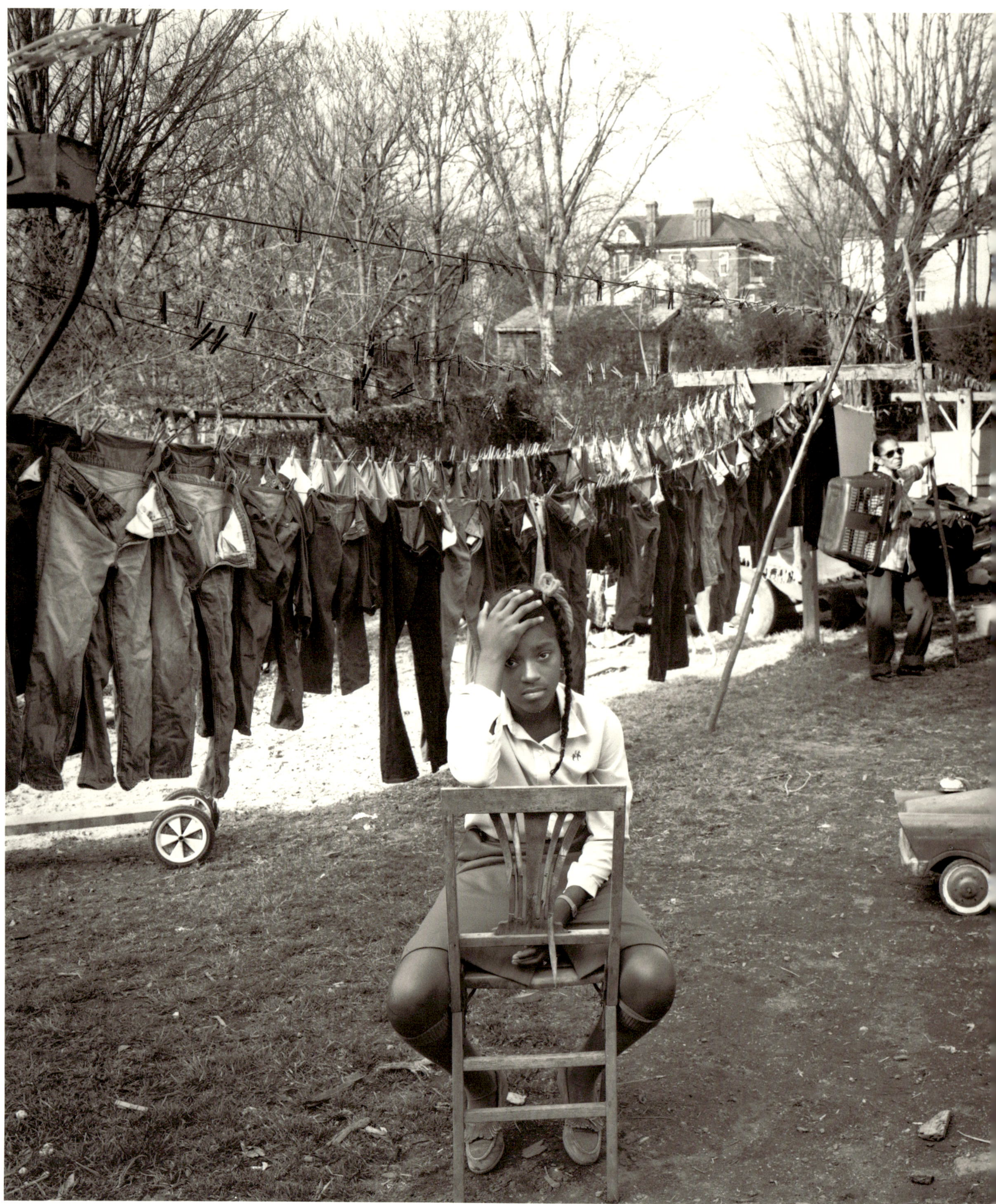

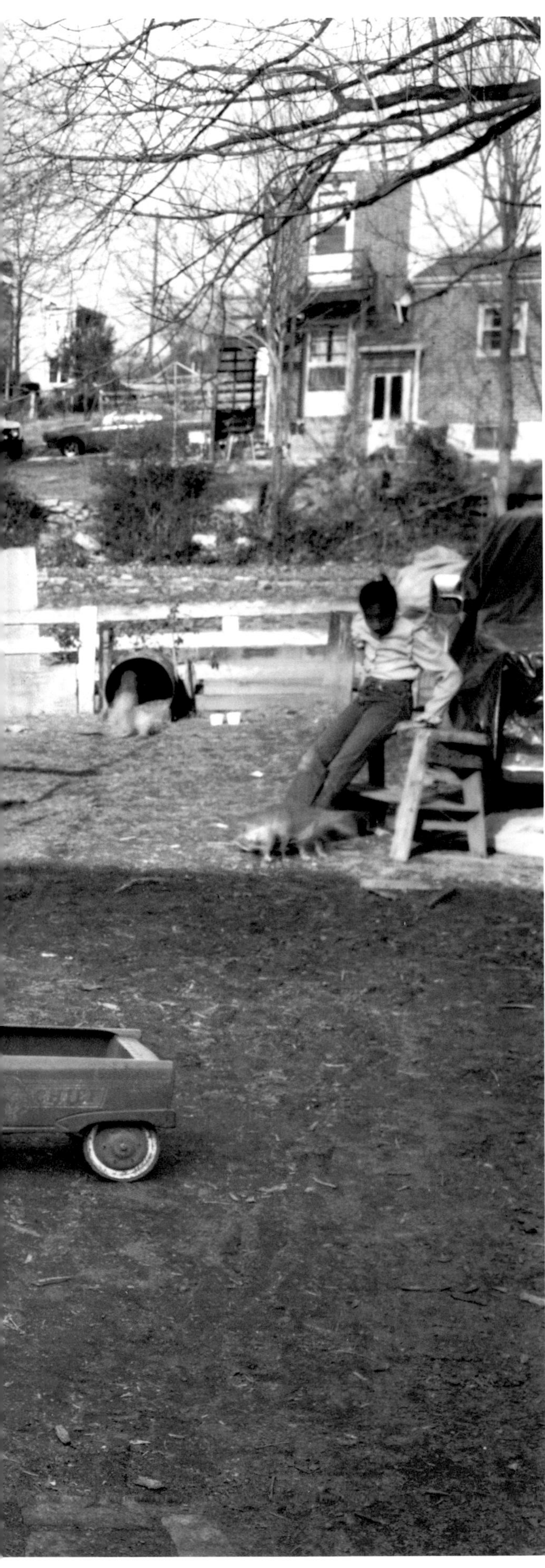

Olivia's face, with that ruined prayer in her eyes, almond eyes, almost Egyptian.

I asked Olivia's grandmother where those eyes came from. She replied that she'd looked carefully at all her daughter's boyfriends that fall when her daughter was fifteen and pregnant with Olivia. And she has looked at them ever since. None of them has eyes like that. Olivia's mother never told.

She didn't stay, either. When she left, Olivia was six months old. But she went on to have three more children; one died and "welfare took the others." I asked the grandmother where Olivia's mother is now, and she said, "She travels."

This is just half of the day's laundry. Olivia joined her grandmother's ten other children. When she was four years old, she, in turn, was joined by an infant cousin whose older sister had been beaten to death by his mother's boyfriend. His mother was traveling, too.

But there had been love and endurance in that crowded family to nourish Olivia. As I sat in the kitchen with the children drifting in and out, I watched her as she watched me. It was as if she too had already traveled out into the world, fostered alike by beauty and by fear.

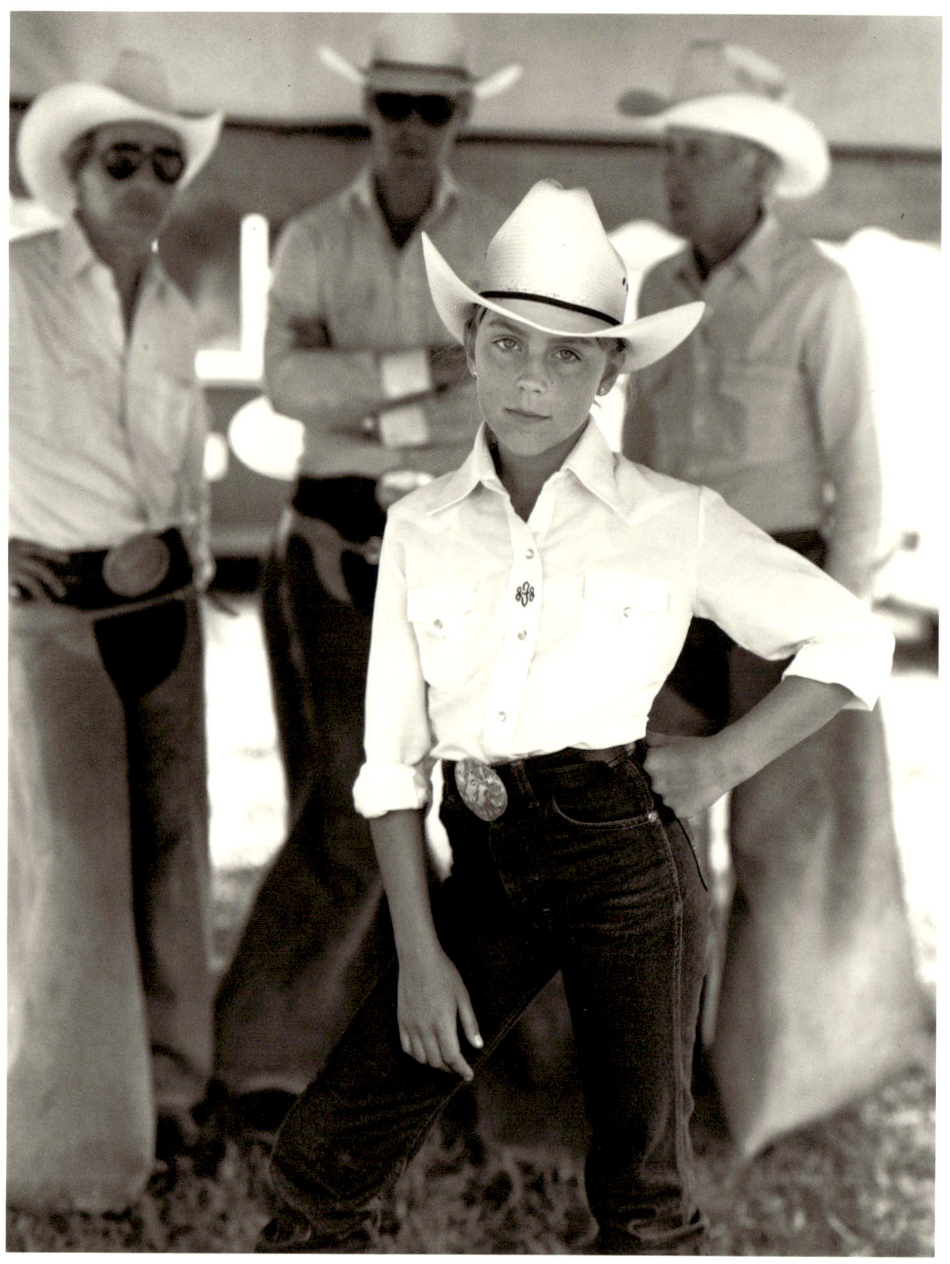

This child was distinctly reluctant to stand closer to her mother's boyfriend. This seemed strange to me, as it was their peculiar familiarity that had provoked this photograph in the first place. Looking through the ground glass I fretted over cropping her elbow but she would not budge toward him.

Several months later her mother shot him in the face with a .22. She testified that while she worked nights at a local truckstop he was "at home partying and harassing my daughter." The child put it to me somewhat more directly. I look at this photograph now with a jaggy chill of realization.

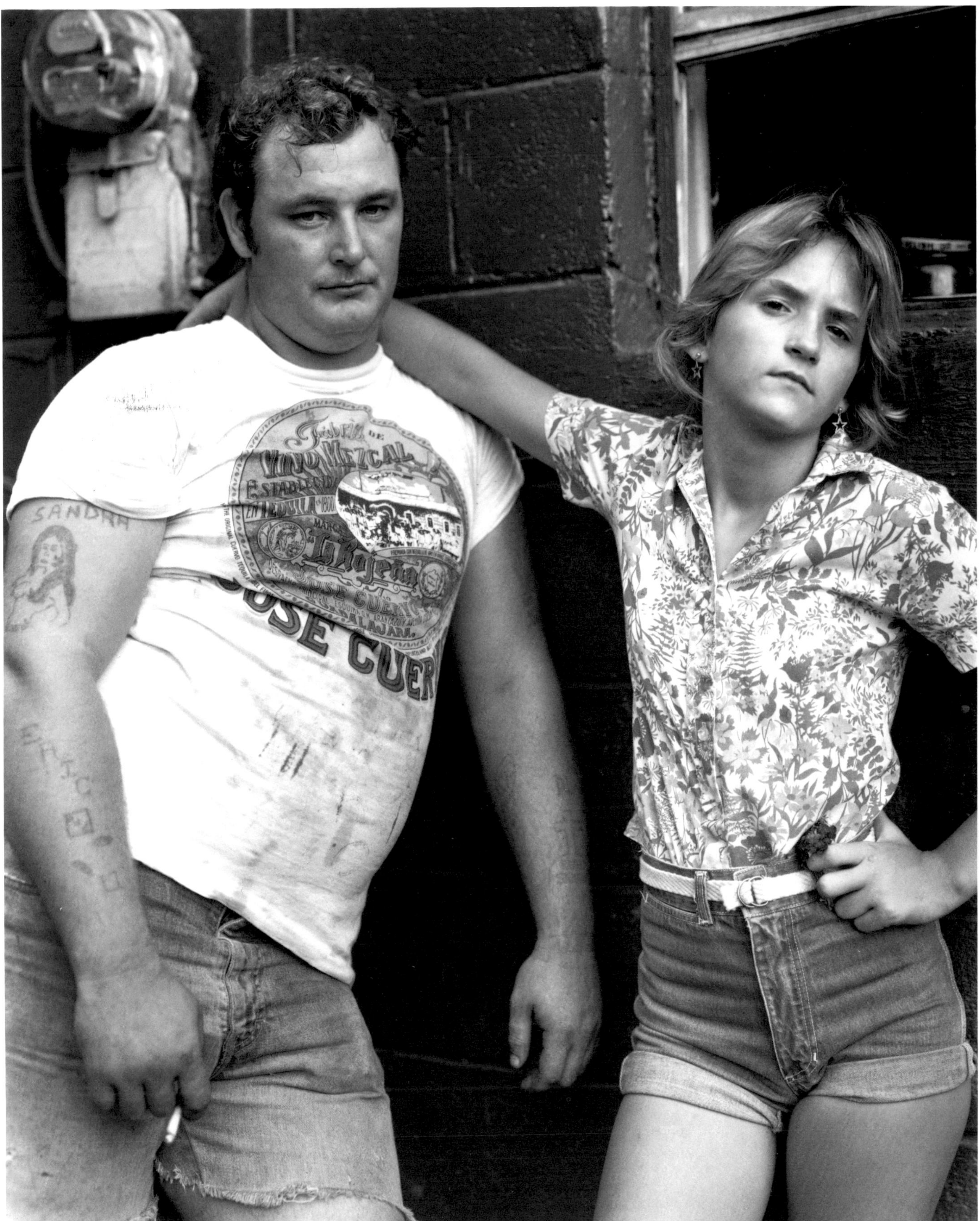
SANDRA
VINO MEZCAL
La Rojeña

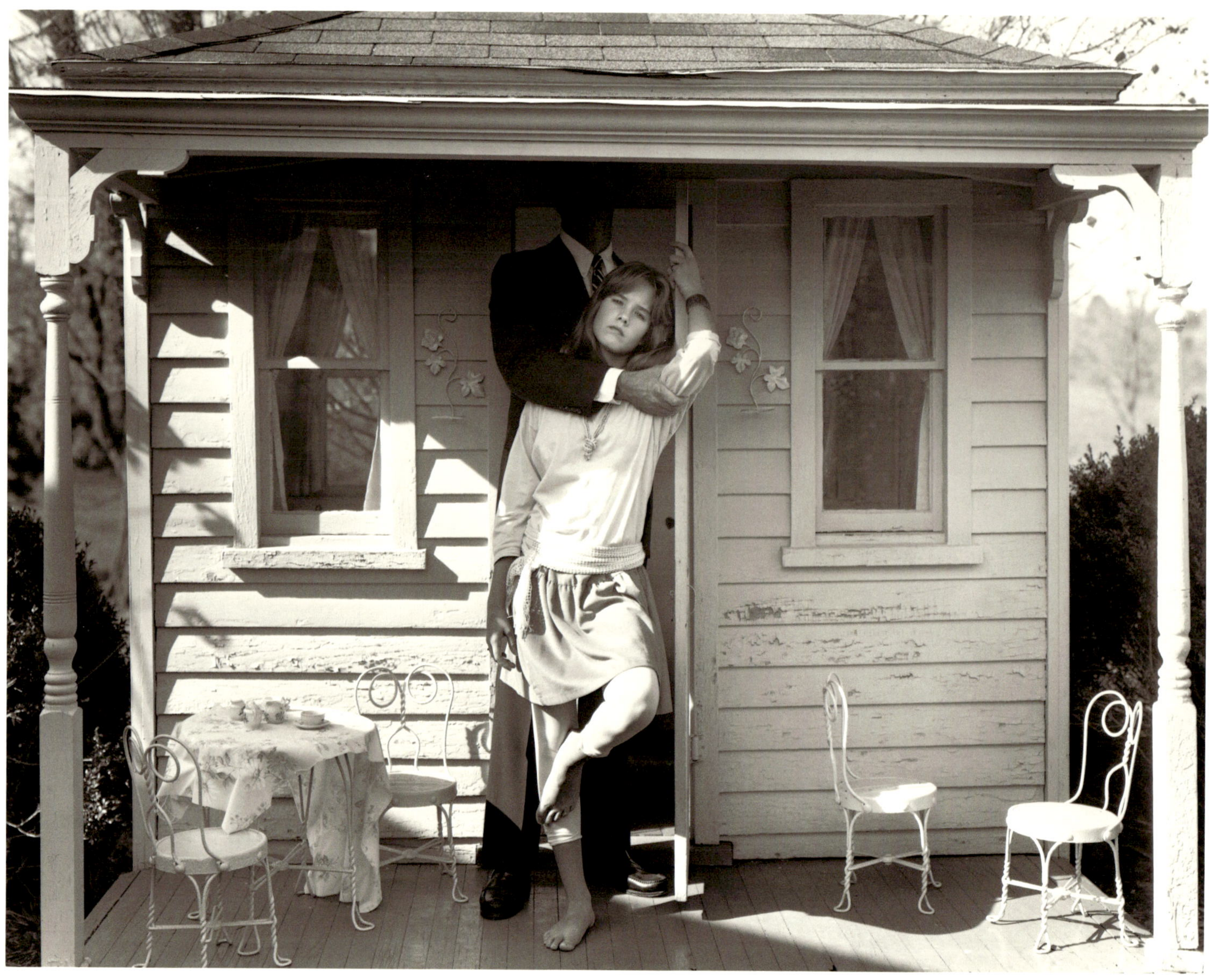

Lewis Carroll wrote that a girl of twelve is one on whom no shadow of sin has fallen, but one who has been touched by the "outermost fringe of the shadow of sorrow."

As with so many of these girls, this child's life has been touched by more than a penumbral fringe of sorrow. This picture of her and her father proved disturbingly prophetic; her eyes sibylline, foreboding.

Repeatedly, I found girls like her who, despite the protective postures that their parents and society assume, already have begun to shoulder the weight of adult reality.

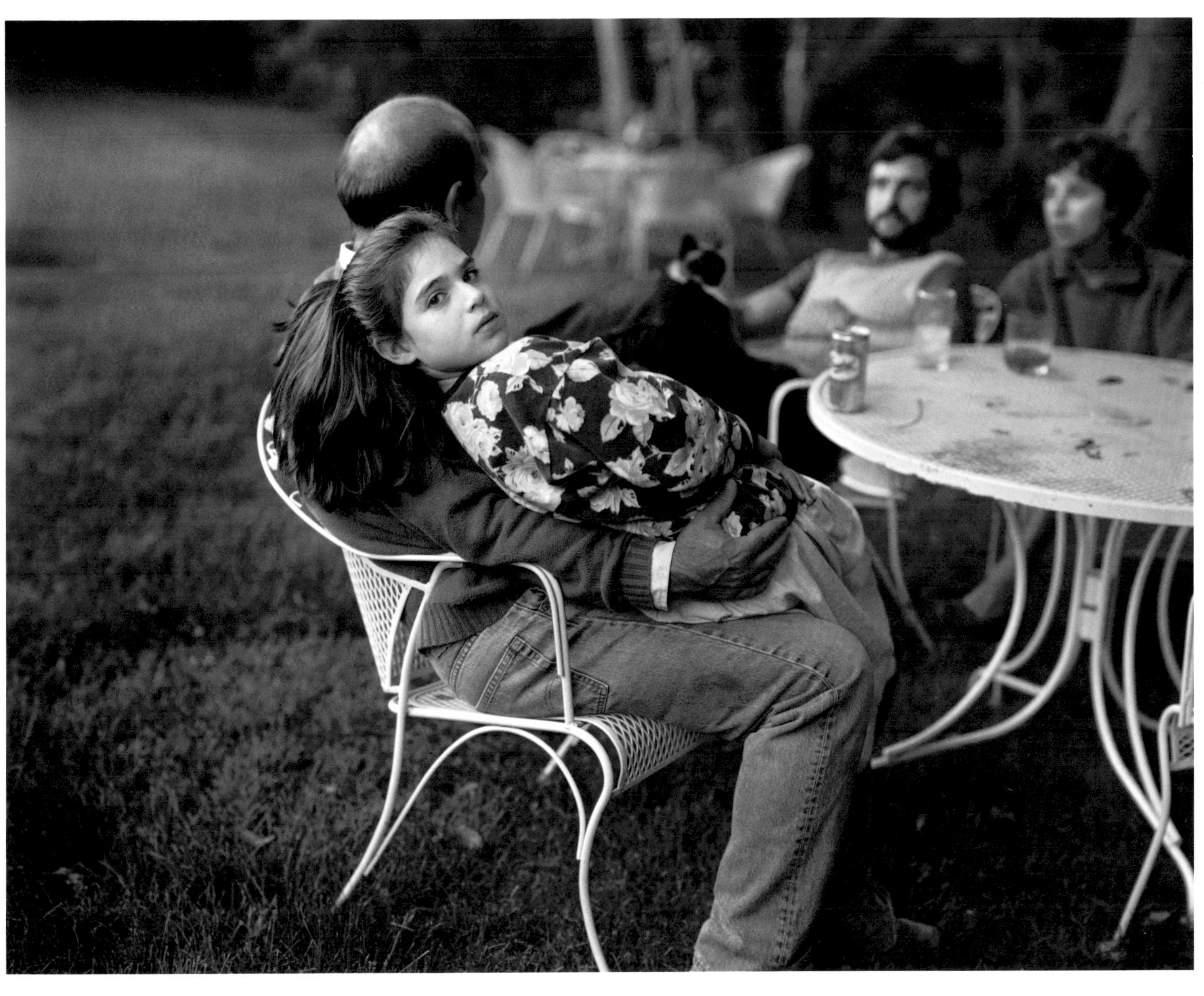

Words seem presumptuous here, for there are so many people and such a great debt. But, with the certain knowledge of the inadequacy of these thanks, I would like to offer my gratitude to all the parents and the children who so willingly participated in this project.

Grateful thanks as well to Ronald Winston, my gentle friend, for his gracious support and infectious confidence; to the John Simon Guggenheim Foundation for their timely and generous Fellowship; and to Frances and Sidney Lewis whose years of interest and support of this book are deeply valued.

I am indebted to my editor Steve Dietz for his subtle manipulation and perfect eye, to Christy Hale, for her excellent design, and to Stevan Baron, Michael Hoffman, and the staff at Aperture. I owe particular thanks to Steve Stinehour for his patience, good humor, and countless bar tabs; and to The Stinehour Press for their uncompromisingly high standards.

Finally, for their enduring support and editorial input over the years, I wish to thank my friends and family, most particularly my parents, Bob and Betty Munger, and Hunter Mohring, Karen Bailey, and Ted Orland.